YACHTING
A Pictorial History

YACHTING
A
Pictorial History

Peter Heaton

A Studio Book
THE VIKING PRESS
New York

preceding pages:
*Masthead view shows orderly deck
of* Nefertiti, *American 12-metre
yacht.*

Copyright© *1972 by Peter
Heaton*

All rights reserved

Published in 1973 by
The Viking Press, Inc.
625 Madison Avenue,
New York, N.Y. 10022

Published simultaneously in
Canada by The Macmillan
Company of Canada Limited

SBN 670-79227-6

Library of Congress catalog card
number: 72-89562

*Printed and bound in Italy by
Arnoldo Mondadori Editore,
Verona*

PICTURE EDITOR
Derek Stevens

PICTURE CREDITS
Cover Ernst Haas   Title Page George Silk, Time-Life
National Maritime Museum—pages 6, 9, 10, 11, 12-13,
14-15 (bottom), 17 (bottom), 19, 20-21, 23 (bottom),
24-25, 28-29, 32, 33, 36, 37, 41   Nederlandsch His-
torisch Scheepvaart Museum, Amsterdam—7   Royal
Thames Yacht Club—15 (top)   Royal Cork Yacht
Club—17 (top)   Beken of Cowes—23 (top), 35 (top),
38, 39, 42, 43, 46 (top), 47 (top and bottom left), 48, 49
(bottom), 52, 53, 54 (bottom), 55, 56, 57, 58-59, 60-61,
62-63, 64-65, 68, 70, 71 (top right), 73-74, 75-78, 79, 80,
and 81, 82, 83 (bottom), 84, 85, 89, 90 (bottom), 91
(*Mapleleaf IV*), 92 (bottom), 95, 108 (top), 109 (top),
116-117, 119, 130, 131 (bottom), 134 (top), 135, 146
(bottom), 150-151, 152 (top), 153, 154-155, 148-149
Culver Pictures—26 (left), 45 (top), 66   Morris
Rosenfeld and Sons—26, 31, 35 (bottom), 44, 47
(bottom right), 49 (top), 50, 51, 55, 67, 71 (bottom
left), 83 (top), 85 (bottom right), 86, 88, 91 (*Miss
America* and Gar Wood), 92 (top), 93, 94, 104 (bottom
right), 96-97, 98, 99, 101 (top), 102, 103, 118   The
Peabody Museum of Salem—27   Radio Times Hulton
Picture Library—46 (bottom), 54 (top), 90 (top), 91
(*Bluebird*), 94 (bottom left)   Laurence Bagley—87
Transworld Features Inc.—100, 128, 129, 146, 147
David Beal—101 (bottom)   Freddie Dalgety—104-105
John Watney—104 (bottom), 118   Gordon Yeldham
—106 (bottom right), 107, 108 (bottom), 110-111
Eileen Ramsay: J. Allan Cash—106, 131 (top), 152
(bottom)   Keystone—109 (bottom)   Gerry Cranham
—111 (top), 112 (bottom), 114-115, 122 (top), 127
Daily Telegraph—112 (top)   Sunday Times—120, 121,
122 (bottom), 123, 124 (bottom), 125, 126   Associated
Press—124 (top)   Oxford University Press—125 (bottom right)   London Express—132, 133, 134 (bottom),
136, 137-138, 139-142   ITV News—143-145

CONTENTS

ORIGINS and DEFINITIONS

A Royal Yacht of Stuart times: the Fubbs, *painted by William van de Velde the younger. The* Fubbs, *148 tons, was built by Phineas Pett at Greenwich in 1682.*

Departure of William and Princess Mary from Gravesend. The picture well illustrates Court yachts of the period.

What is a yacht? At first sight an easy question; it grows in complexity. The definition is elusive. Most people have some idea what is meant by the word yacht, but these ideas are many and varied. The dandified Carruthers in Erskine Childers' book *The Riddle of the Sands*, found on being introduced to Davies' yacht *Dulcibella* that this tough and weather-worn little vessel did not measure up to *his* conception of a yacht at all: '. . . Hazily there floated through my mind my last embarkation on a yacht; my faultless attire, the trim gig and obsequious sailors, the accommodation ladder flashing with varnish and brass in the August sun, the orderly snowy decks and basket chairs under the awning aft. What a contrast with this sordid midnight scramble, over damp meat and littered packing cases! The bitterest touch of all was a growing sense of inferiority and ignorance, which I had never before been allowed to feel in my experience of yachts'.

Earlier in the same book Carruthers' viewpoint (and the viewpoint of many like him) is convincingly expressed as he re-reads Davies' letter of invitation '. . . yachting in the Baltic at the end of September; the very idea made one shudder. Cowes, with a pleasant party and hotels handy, was all very well'. And later again, on trying to recall what he had heard recently of Davies '. . . I had always connected him with boats and the sea, but never with yachting'.

The contrast between the well-appointed yacht at Cowes and the tough little converted lifeboat in which Davies had made his way to the Baltic Fjords can be extended further. For example: compare the dedicated dinghy racing man who every weekend competes with literally hundreds of other similar dinghies (frequently car-trailing his dinghy home at the end of the day) with the 'glamour' kind of yachting visualized in Monaco harbour by the American writer David Dodge. In *The Rich Man's Guide to the Riviera* Dodge slyly evokes the pretentious pleasure of lying between silken sheets aboard your own luxurious vessel knowing '. . . that Ari and the Môme and the Maharani and Karim and Hapsie-Pooh and Nam and Juanito and the rest of your friends are moored all around you in *their* yachts . . .'

Then there is the strictly practical approach, the 'do it all yourself' man. There are many yachtsmen who are as happy (perhaps happier) laying the keel of a vessel than actually sailing her. There is the purely romantic approach; that, for example of Uffa Fox, in *According to Uffa*: '. . . Enjoy the soul-satisfying pleasure of sailing the seas, lakes and rivers of this earth, traversing its wide waters without any noise except the clink, clink, clink of the waves and the swish of the seas as they are cleft by our vessel's cut-water'.

The romantic concept is out of fashion today. Most people were intrigued more by the navigational expertise and physical endurance of Sir Francis Chichester than by the romantic aspect of his solitary circumnavigation in the yacht *Gipsy Moth IV*. Patrick Boyle in his entertaining book *Sailing in a Nutshell* disposes of the romantic concept in a definition of 'yacht', more subtle than it might first appear, as '. . . a ship, vessel, craft, bottom, packet, floating palace, hooker or whatnot, intended for navigating seas, rivers, canals, lakes or ornamental water for pleasure, exercise, fresh air, to impress one's friend's or to elude the rates'.

The very first single-handed circumnavigator in a yacht was Captain Joshua Slocum, who sailed the *Spray* round the world, flying the Stars and Stripes and navigating by a tin clock bought for a dollar. Can that professional sea captain be described as a 'yachtsman'? There are those who hold that the *Spray* was not a yacht at all. A recently published dictionary gives the following definition: 'A vessel built for private pleasure sailing and not plying for hire'. This would seem to leave many questions unanswered. The *Concise Oxford Dictionary* is anything but concise in its definition of 'yacht' '. . . 1. Light sailing vessel kept, and usually specially built and rigged for racing; vessel propelled by sails, steam, electricity, or motive power other than oars, and used for private pleasure excursions, cruising, travel, etcetera'. A fuller definition still was given by Falconer in his *Marine Dictionary* of 1771 in which a yacht is described as '. . . a vessel of state, normally employed to convey princes, ambassadors or other great personages from one kingdom to another . . . as the principal design of a yacht is to accommodate the passengers, it is usually fitted with a variety of convenient apartments, with suitable furniture, according to the quality or number of persons contained therein. The Royal Yachts are commonly rigged as Ketches, except the principal one reserved for the sovereign which is equipped with three masts like a ship. They are in general elegantly furnished and nobly ornamented with sculpture, and always commanded by Captains in His Majesty's Navy. Besides these, there are many other yachts of a smaller kind, employed by the commissioners of excise, navy and customs; or used as pleasure boats by private gentlemen'.

This would seem to leave us in little doubt as to what was meant by a yacht in 1771. When this definition was given, yachts had already been in existence in England for a century, since in fact, the time of the Restoration of King Charles II, in 1660. It is clear from Falconer's definition that the word yacht still meant principally a vessel of state used by exalted personages for waterborne ceremonies attended by much pomp and ritual. However something new had been introduced by Charles, the sport of yacht racing, and which marked the difference between yachting in England and yachting in Holland.

Falconer's definition would seem to have little relevance today. Yachts as vessels of state have largely ceased to exist. A few remain: the British Royal Yacht, the yacht of the President of the United States of America, and the King of

The Stuart Royal yacht Mary.

7

Norway's yacht, to name three. Today the pleasure function has outstripped the state function almost completely. The use of the word yacht in connection with vessels of the customs and commissioners of excise has disappeared. Although there are in existence vessels of state which come within the definition of a yacht, the emphasis has shifted.

Vessels of state have existed from time immemorial. Cleopatra was borne in such a craft at the battle of Actium. The *Isis* and the *Thelamegus* both built by Ptolemy Philopator (222 BC) were two more of the same class of vessel. The galley of Hardicanute, 'sumptuously gilt and rowed by eighty men, six of whom wore on his arm a bracelet of gold weighing sixteen ounces' (AD 1040) was another. One could continue adding to the list: the brilliant galleys of Venice with their gold and silver embroidered sails; the sumptuous craft of Spain and Portugal; the slender, beautiful vessels of the raiding Norsemen; some of these were used as vessels of state. In England vessels of state appear from time to time in early records. One such was the 'vessel with purple sails' given by the King of Norway to Athelstan the Saxon king of England in AD 925. Another was the pleasure ship *Rat of Wight*, built in 1588 for Queen Elizabeth at Cowes.

Yachting as we know it today however, and as practised by the general run of what we may term 'yachtsmen', which includes racing and cruising and the social function of the 'yacht club', is a development from the original Dutch conception. The word yacht is a Dutch word: in a Dutch-Latin dictionary published at Antwerp in 1599, the word yacht 'jaght' is shown as having its root in 'jaghen' meaning 'to hunt or to pursue'. It is also shown as having a secondary meaning, which is to tow a vessel (and so increase her speed) with horses. From this developed the slang word 'jaghten' meaning to hurry or quicken, and also the word 'jaght' used in connection with chasing or hunting. In the same dictionary 'jaght, jaghte, or jaght schip' are given as meaning a swift, light-built vessel of war, a ship which, probably designed in the first instance for naval use, came to be used also for commerce and pleasure.

The Dutch did not race their yachts, but by the seventeenth century they were using them for many other purposes. There were yachts employed on Government business; passenger-carrying yachts; Admiralty yachts in the service of the Navy; dispatch yachts and many privately owned yachts, magnificently painted, sporting lofty sterns and high bowsprits, belonging to the wealthy citizens of Amsterdam, Rotterdam and other towns. From the very nature of the country, yachting was the most serviceable and much the pleasantest means of transport in the Netherlands in the seventeenth century. Yachts were almost an essential of life in a country where water was always nearby; but in addition to the

everyday use of their yachts the Dutch held frequent aquatic parades, usually in imitation of naval battles.

When Peter the Great visited Amsterdam in 1697 the yachts of that city gave one of these displays and an account of this was published in the same year.

By the beginning of the seventeenth century the Netherlands had reached a considerable state of affluence, and King Charles I of England's demand as Sovereign of the seas for £30,000 annually for the licence to fish in the narrow seas was a not unreasonable imposition. The growing maritime activity of Holland was one of the most remarkable developments that Europe had seen. It is recorded that in 1560 fifteen hundred herring boats sailed from Dutch ports in the course of three days. In observations made upon Dutch fishing about the year 1601, John Keymor wrote that more wealth was produced by the northern fisheries . . . 'in one year than the King of Spain has in four years out of the Indies'.

As the Dutch nation increased in power and wealth so the number of yachts multiplied. By the middle of the seventeenth century, a yacht was a normal possession of a person of any consequence. Yachting was the 'thing to do'; a social yardstick. It was not surprising that the young Prince Charles, exiled and living on the Continent since he was twenty-one, and who had spent part of that exile in Holland, should have become infected with a taste for yachting.

On 8 May 1660, Charles was pronounced King of England by proclamation in Westminster Hall, London. He himself was still in Holland at Breda. On receipt of this information, the new King set out at once, attended by his court, to make the journey, first from Breda to the Hague, and thence to England. For the first part of this journey the Dutch placed a number of yachts at his disposal and no sooner had the news of the proclamation reached the Prince of Orange than he too contributed a 'beautifully carved and gilded' yacht. This was the vessel which carried Charles from Breda to Rotterdam.

There exists an account of this passage from Breda published in 1660 by Adrien Vlackett . . . 'The yacht on board of which the King sailed had been built for himself by the Prince of Orange, but now belongs to the Board of Admiralty of Rotterdam, and it was without doubt the finest of the little fleet, which consisted, without other ships, almost countless, of thirteen large yachts, which the persons of rank use in the rivers and on the sea, to pass from one province to another, for necessity as well as for pleasure.

'The King found his yacht so convenient and comfortable that he remarked, while discoursing with the Deputies, that he might order one of the same style, so soon as he should arrive in England, to use on the River Thames. Mr. Van Vlooswyck, Burgermaster of Amsterdam, and one of the Deputies of the province of Holland, taking occasion to do a considerable service to

A Dutch Prince's yacht, viewed from the starboard quarter. On the taffrail between two pilasters: a round shield bearing the quartered and inescutcheoned arms of the Prince of Orange, wreathed and crowned and supported by two figures of fame blowing trumpets. On the starboard quarter: a figure of justice holding scales. On the port quarter: a figure holding a shield. The leeboard, and the side down to the second wale, are very elaborately decorated.

The Stuart yacht Kitchen. *Kitchen, 8 guns, was built in 1670, and made a bomb vessel in 1692. Two square decorated ports forward, one amidships, a double light aft and a small badge on the quarter, a lion figurehead.*

The Stuart yacht Charlotte.

*The Lives of the Norths.
†After the Duchess of Portsmouth.

his fatherland, said to the King that lately a yacht had been built in Amsterdam which was almost of the same size, and at least as handsome, and he took the liberty of presenting it to his Majesty'.

In a dictionary of sailing by F. H. Burgess, published as a Penguin reference book, 'yacht' is defined as 'a private pleasure vessel or boat, built specifically for racing or cruising, and with living accommodation for her crew'. There are thousands of yachts which take part in racing; in sheltered water, on reservoirs, lakes, rivers, and in the open sea. But there are probably even more which are used primarily as cruisers, floating movable homes able to satisfy the wanderlust in all men. The practice of racing preceded that of cruising, but only by a few years, for in 1675 we find the Honourable Roger North including in his autobiography* a delightful account, and probably the first one, of a yacht cruise. In 1676, there is an account of a cruise made by King Charles II down the Thames and round the Kentish coast in a Royal Yacht *Fubbs*.†

From such beginnings did the twin sports of racing and cruising develop. For a very long time the cruising yacht and the racing yacht were considered to be two very different species. One was light and fast and over-canvassed; the other heavy, supremely seaworthy and under-canvassed. With the relatively recent development of the sport of ocean racing the two types have merged, and the term 'cruiser-racer' is now in common use as meaning a yacht suitable in all respects for both practices. One of the most extensive postwar developments in sailing has been that of dinghy racing. Is a dinghy a yacht? Referring to Burgess '. . . a private pleasure vessel or boat, built specifically for racing or cruising, and with living accommodation for her crew'. With the spread of dinghy cruising, has come the practice of rigging a tent for protection from the weather at night while asleep. But 'living accommodation' means more than a tent. It implies a cabin, with berths, decked over and providing a permanent fixed shelter. Moreover, Burgess himself defines 'dinghy' . . . 'a small open rowing boat . . . varying from eight to sixteen feet in length, and used for rowing, sailing, fishing, and all utility purposes'. Nevertheless, so many of today's 'yachtsmen' do their racing (and cruising) in dinghies that the dinghy must surely be included. The definition embraces power yachts as well as sail. Outboard racing craft, of which the smallest hydroplanes can not strictly be termed yachts, have been included as well. The small hydroplanes like the racing dinghies, are an important feature of the modern yachting scene. Many personalities have not only enriched the sport with their vitality and enthusiasm but have contributed much to its technical development. Only a relative handful can be mentioned in these pages, but we may at least start with one enthusiast: the King who was instrumental in importing 'yachting' to England.

YACHTS of the STUART COURT

**'Every drop of the
Thames is liquid 'istory.'**
John Burns

*O*nly three months after the Restoration, Samuel Pepys, calling at Whitehall, found 'the King gone this morning by five of the clock to see a Dutch pleasure boat below the Bridge'. The boat in question was the vessel *Mary*, the gift of the city of Amsterdam. The *Mary* typically resembled a warship in miniature carrying eight guns and requiring a crew of thirty men. She was 66 foot long, she had a breadth of 19 feet, a draft of 10 feet and she was 100 tons burden. But Charles had already given the order to his shipwrights to build a new British yacht on similar lines to the *Mary*. On 8 November 1660 Pepys wrote: '. . . in the afternoon Commissioner Pett and I went on board the yacht (*Mary*), which indeed is one of the finest things that I ever saw for neatness and room in so small a vessel. Mister Pett is to make one to outdo this for the honour of his country, which I fear he will scarce better'. The price was not excessive. An entry in the Admiralty papers of 3 November 1660 reads: '. . . estimate by Peter Pett of the charges of building a new yacht of 80 tons for the King at Deptford: total 1,335 pounds sterling'.

The Dutch yachts of which *Mary* was an example were broad-beamed, shallow draft and fitted with lee-boards which helped them to sail to windward better when the depth of water permitted; a type of vessel eminently suitable for the shallow waters of Holland. Charles' attack of sea-fever infected his brother, the Duke of York. Under their patronage shipwrights Peter and Christopher Pett and Thomas Shish modified

the Dutch design to suit the deeper waters around England, and between 1661 and 1663 designed and built five Royal Yachts. The King and his brother particularly enjoyed racing for wagers. Recording a race, the diarist John Evelyn wrote . . . 'October 1st 1661. I had sailed this morning with His Majesty in one of the yachts or pleasure boats . . . being very excellent sailing vessels. It was on a wager between his other new pleasure boat, built frigate-like, and one of the Duke of York's; the wager one hundred pounds sterling; the race from Greenwich to Gravesend and back. The King lost in going, the wind being contrary, but saved stakes in returning. There were divers noble persons and lords on board, his Majesty sometimes steering himself. His barge and kitchen boat attended. I break fast this morning with the King at return in his smaller vessel, he being pleased to take me and only four more, who were noblemen, with him; but dined in his yacht where we ate together with his Majesty'. The fashion started by the King spread. By July 1663 Christopher Pett was asking for '. . . a gratuity for building the pleasure boats, as he has to entertain so many people'. Charles' enthusiasm for the sport indeed led Pepys, as secretary at the Admiralty, to complain of the King's extravagance. The Royal Yachts were paid for out of the Privy Purse and at one time there were no less than fifteen; the largest being the 133 ton *Portsmouth*; so Pepys may have had a point. There was however, another side to the picture. As soon as the King tired of a yacht it was immediately made available for service with

Sheer plan of a yacht for the van de Veldes—port side. Note the large companion hatch added in pencil.

the Navy, for Charles' enthusiasm for yachting was equalled by his interest in Naval architecture and his determination that England should be a great sea power. It seems that inflation has always dogged yacht building. Each successive Royal Yacht cost more. In place of coarse French canvas, sails were cut from Holland duck. The use of lead ballast was a further extravagance, and there was much gilding and carving both on bow and stern and below decks. But although during the ten years 1660 to 1670, the King and his brother and to some extent his court, had shown great initial interest in yachting there was no general development in the country. After the first enthusiasm the yachting boom collapsed. (The outbreak of the Dutch war in 1665, when all Royal pleasure vessels were turned over to the Navy and pleasure sailing ceased, to some extent accounted for this.)

After the death of King Charles II in 1685, yachting, having lost its patron, was to decline still further and during the reign of James II no new boats were commissioned. James was succeeded after a short reign, by William III, a Dutchman, and his wife Mary. Although William rekindled moderate interest in yachting, he did not have the enthusiasm of Charles II. He did, however, bring with him from Holland a remarkable vessel although not a 'yacht', for use as one, called *Princess Mary*. She had been built in Holland in about 1677, was 80 feet 3 inches in length and 23 feet broad, and had two decks. She must have been extremely well built for she lasted for 139 years. She was used as a Royal Yacht by

William, Queen Anne and George I. By order of the latter in 1714 she ceased to form part of the Royal establishment and led a somewhat chequered existence playing the role of a West Indiaman, Smyrna figger, and privateer. She was present at the siege of Cadiz and did service for a time as headquarters of the Royal Marine Artillery. She ended her long life as a collier, a fact which inspired Doctor Sheldon McKenzie to write:
'Behold the fate of sublunary things:
She exports coal which once imported Kings'.

In 1698 Peter the Great visited England. The Czar was an enthusiastic yachtsman and Macaulay records that 'the only Englishman of rank in whose society he seemed to take much pleasure was the eccentric Caermarthen, whose passion for the sea bore some resemblance to his own, and who was very competent to give an opinion about every part of a ship from the stem to the stern'. It is clear from contemporary accounts that the Czar had a genuine interest in yachts as yachts. The monarchs who followed Charles II had not; neither William and Mary, nor Queen Anne; and the early Georges had little use for yachts except as a means of returning to Europe and the country of their birth.

With the accession of George III yachting came back into favour; the King using yachts for Naval reviews, marine excursions and visits to the fleet at Spithead. Royal yachts had now to be 'bigger and better'. In 1803 a new yacht of 350 tons was built, named *Royal Sovereign* and described as 'far exceeding any other of her kind'.

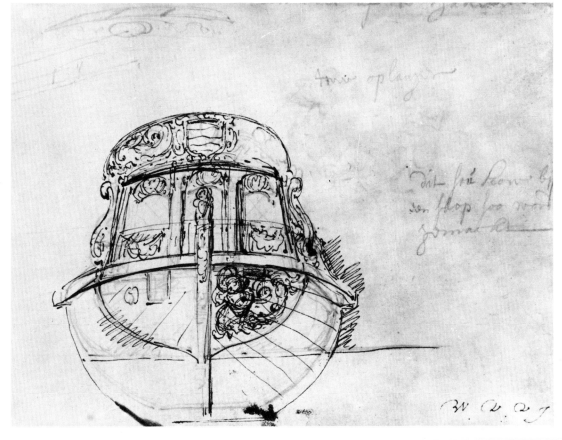

Sketch drawing of the stern of a yacht to be built for the van de Veldes. It shows a stern in the form of three arches, referred to by the inscription 'twee oplanger', and dolphins head downwards at quarter pieces, referred to by the inscription 'op sij dun'. On the rail above: van de Velde's arms supported by dolphins; the transom is also decorated.

pages 12 and 13:
The Royal Yacht Sovereign *under full sail, with Queen Charlotte on board, leaving Portsmouth to review a Russian Squadron.*

THE FIRST YACHT CLUBS

'We were the first that
ever burst into that
silent sea.'
S. T. Coleridge

Painted by J. Kitchingman

To His Royal Highness
DUKE of CUMBERLAND,
This PLATE representing the different Sailing Boats belonging
With a View of the Fort at SHEERNESS and
Is by Permission most humbly Inscribed.

Published as the Act directs June 1 1778.

The Duke of Cumberland.

Yachts of the Cumberland Fleet off the entrance to the River Medway.

During the eighteenth century the sport of yachting, although given little encouragement in Royal circles, had spread to the ordinary citizen. It is in Ireland that one finds the first forbear of that esoteric institution, the Yacht Club. In 1720 the Water Club of the harbour of Cork was founded, consisting of 25 members. Their practice was to cruise in company under an Admiral whose pleasure it was to hoist signals controlling (at least in theory) the movements of his fleet.

The artist Peter Monamy, who enjoyed a considerable vogue as a landscape and marine painter in the early part of the eighteenth century, painted a number of pictures of the Water Club fleet. The vessels may be seen as solidly built, bluff-bowed cutters, similar to the type of craft in current use by Pilots, Revenue officers and smugglers. The members of the Club wore splendid uniforms. They had extensive rules and records of their activities were lovingly kept. A good deal of eating and drinking was done as well as sailing. Rule number 27 in the Rules and Orders dated 1765 reads '... Resolved. That each member (unless out of the Kingdom) entertains in his turn, or substitutes a member in his room otherwise the Secretary is to provide a dinner, the cost of which is to be paid by the member whose turn it shall be to attend, on pain of expulsion'.

The year 1765 marks not only the list of rules at their most prolix but also the end of the Club. At the beginning of the nineteenth century an attempt was made to revive it. A small number of survivors of the old Water Club formed the Little Monkstown Club. The revival may be said to have succeeded, since later the right to the title of the Royal Cork Yacht Club was granted to the members, and as such the Club exists to this day. It can claim to be the oldest yacht club in the world, with only one dissenting voice, that of Russia.

The Russian claim to have founded the first yacht club in the world is supported by a book entitled *The Sport of Sailing in U.S.S.R.* published in 1954 and written by N. V. Grigorieff and B. B. Lobatch-Joutchenko. In it the authors state that the first yacht club was founded in Russia by Peter the First in 1718 under the name of the Flotilla of the Neva. It was formed to encourage 'a taste for navigation, to spread nautical knowledge and to give service men and their children a taste for the sea'.

Peter the First made available one hundred and forty vessels free to divers people, to sail and 'instruct themselves in the conduct of these vessels'. The vessels are described as 'yachts in the actual meaning of the word'.

This claim to be the oldest club rests on the fact that the Flotilla of the Neva had its own flag and that the vessels were 'yachts in the actual meaning of the word'. It is not clear, however, to what extent they could be termed 'pleasure vessels' as sailing them would appear to be something of a duty imposed by Peter the First who had provided the vessels for the purposes mentioned. Whatever else, the matter is certainly a pregnant subject for Yacht Club fireside debate.

It is not recorded that the members of the Cork Water Club indulged in racing. Indeed with their marine excursions and manoeuvring under their Admiral they may be said to have something in common with the quasi-Naval activities and mock battles of some of the early Dutch yachtsmen. But in the latter part of the eighteenth century the racing element was to come back on the waters where it had made its first appearance under the patronage of Charles II—the River Thames. The founding of the Cumberland Fleet, the ancestor of the present-day Royal Thames Yacht Club, takes us nearer to yachting as we know it. The Water Club yachtsmen made 'excursions'. The members of the Cumberland Fleet did the same but they also raced. As early as 1749 a race had been sailed from Greenwich to the Nore and back, for a plate presented by the Prince of Wales. With the advent of Henry Frederick Duke of Cumberland as patron of the fleet which took his name, the sport of yacht racing may be said to have had its beginnings, for several vessels, rather than two or three, took part, and raced under definite rules. The Regattas were held between Blackfriars and Putney. Apart from its distinguished patron, the members of the fleet were predominantly commoners; professional men who kept craft at Temple Stairs and businessmen and merchants whose houses fronted the river along Chelsea reach. To mark the coronation of King George IV the name of the fleet was changed in 1823 to His Majesty's Coronation Society. The life of this Society was short. Its first race resulted in a protest case and the findings of the committee were bitterly disputed. Some members drawn together by common disagreement and indignation met at the White House Tavern and there formed the Thames Yacht Club, the true forerunner of today's Royal Thames Yacht Club. The vessels of the Cumberland fleet flew the White Ensign, but without the red cross of St. George. The yachts of the Fleet cruised as well as raced. In 1777 one of them, the *Hawke,* was chased into Calais by an American privateer, while she was cruising in the English Channel. The fleet yachts were beamy, bluff-bowed, rigged mainly as cutters, with gaff mainsail, staysail and jib on a long bowsprit. (Some of the larger vessels set topsails.) Racing in the Thames, heeled over under their three working sails, they must have made a brave sight tacking across the green-fringed blue of the London river on a summer's day.

Although organized yacht racing had begun with the merchants and businessmen of London it was not long before a fresh wind was to blow from a more aristocratic quarter. The scene is another tavern; this time the Thatched House in St. James' Street, London. The date is 1 June

Yacht of the Cork Water Club, ancestor of the present Royal Cork Yacht Club and the oldest yacht club in the world.

Lord Yarborough's yacht Falcon *(351 tons) off Spithead with other yachts of the Royal Yacht Squadron on their way to Cherbourg. Painted by W. J. Huggins.*

1815. Meeting under the chairmanship of Lord Grantham, a number of nobles and gentlemen founded a new club, styled, with misleading simplicity, The Yacht Club. Off to a good start, the new club gathered impressive way. Two years later at a meeting at East Cowes, Sir Arthur Paget read a letter written by the Prince Regent intimating his wish to join the club. The following year the Dukes of Clarence and Gloucester became members and when in 1820 the Regent became King George IV, the club, with his permission, could style itself the Royal Yacht Club.

George IV, whose patronage had created Brighton as a fashionable resort, was in some respects to do the same thing for Cowes and the Solent. But the Solent with its particularly suitable geography was rapidly to become a great yachting centre.

The Isle of Wight already had a long history as a pleasure resort. It was occupied by the Romans who called it Vectis or Vecta. Cowes was known as Cowe or Cows and the Solent as the Solent Sea from the Latin *Solvendo*. Later, the Normans also liked the place, and a relative of the Conqueror, William FitzOsborne, was given the lordship of the Island. In 1540 two forts were built; one on each side of the entrance to the Medina River. The fort on the eastern side disappeared by 1610 but that on the west still stands. For many years it was the residence of the Governor of the Island, until, renovated and altered, it became what it is today: the home of the Royal Yacht Squadron.

It was not the Royal Yacht Club's first home in the Isle of Wight. In 1824 a committee of the Club, under the chairmanship of Lord Yarborough, recommended the acquisition of the lease of a house on the Parade at Cowes. This house, the first residence of the Royal Yacht Club, is today well known as the Gloster Hotel. In the same year (1824) Lord Yarborough was elected the club's first Commodore. Most of the members of the Royal Yacht Club were not merely aristocratic, they were rich. Lord Yarborough's own vessel *Falcon* of 351 tons, and typical of one of the larger yachts of the period, was full rigged and, maintaining the tradition (although not the appearance) of the Stuart yachts, resembled a miniature warship. In the first meetings of the Royal Yacht Club there was little suggestion of racing; the first gatherings being more like the aquatic exhibitions associated with the early days of yachting. However, as far back as 1815, two members, Mr. Joseph Weld and Mr. Thomas Assheton-Smith, had what was to be the first of many races. This race took place at Cowes. Mr. Weld's yacht was the 65-ton cutter *Charlotte,* Mr. Assheton-Smith's was the *Elizabeth* of the same tonnage. The wager was 500 guineas and the *Hampshire Telegraph* reported it in full. *Elizabeth* lost her mast-head and Mr. Weld had the satisfaction not only of winning the race but of towing his defeated rival back to Cowes. One of these contests is of particular

interest as being probably the first race round the Isle of Wight (on 24 July 1824) between Mr. James Weld's 43-ton yawl *Julia* and Mr. C. R. M. Talbot's yawl *Giulia* of 42 tons. Although these two vessels were of approximately the same size, yet in these early races competing craft were often very unevenly matched; a relatively small vessel of about 85 tons, such as Mr. Joseph Weld's cutter *Arrow,* taking on Mr. Assheton-Smith's 140-ton schooner *Jack O'Lantern.* There was considerable rivalry and a good deal of bad temper. In 1829 Mr. Assheton-Smith's *Menai,* Mr. Weld's *Lulworth* and Lord Belfast's *Louisa* took part in a race in which *Louisa* and *Lulworth* collided. The crew of *Louisa* drew cutlasses and cut away some of *Lulworth's* running rigging. Mr. Weld protested vainly against Lord Belfast. In another race *Louisa* ran into Mr. Assheton-Smith's *Menai.* As far as the latter was concerned, all this extrovert behaviour at sea had a significant result from the point of view of yachting history, for Mr. Assheton-Smith was so upset by it that he stopped racing. Indeed he did more. 'Perplexed and distressed' like Lewis Carroll's Bellman, he agreed that 'the principal failing occurred in the sailing'. He gave up sailing and began to build steam yachts, commissioning nine large craft between 1830 and 1850. But steam yachts were regarded as even more ungentlemanly than hand-to-hand fighting during races, and resulted in Mr. Assheton-Smith leaving the Royal Yacht Club.

In 1829 a new system of handicapping had been introduced: dividing yachts into six classes according to tonnage. The first class gave to the second a distance of half a mile over a forty mile course. The third class was given one and a quarter miles; the fourth two and a quarter and so on. The smallest class (the sixth) received seven miles. It certainly introduced an element of fairness and ended the supremacy of the larger yachts.

By 1830 and the accession to the throne of King William IV, the Royal Yacht Club was established as a powerful influence in all yachting matters. In 1829 a warrant had been issued by the Admiralty granting to members of the Royal Yacht Club the privilege of flying the White Ensign from their yachts as long as they were on board. In 1833 a further distinction was bestowed when the following letter was received by the Secretary:

Sir, I have it in command from His Majesty to acquaint you, for the information of the Commodore and the Officers of the Royal Yacht Club, that as a mark of His Majesty's gracious approval of an institution of such National utility, it is his gracious wish and pleasure that it shall be henceforth known and styled 'The Royal Yacht Squadron', of which His Majesty is graciously pleased to consider himself the head.
Signed, Belfast.

It was appropriate that the letter should bear

Cutter yacht Elizabeth—*built about 1815.*

Schooner yacht Czarina *(210 tons) built in 1853.*

the signature of Lord Belfast, the owner of *Louisa* (whose crew had fought Mr. Weld's *Lulworth* and which had collided with Mr. Assheton-Smith's *Menai*). Lord Belfast was a remarkable man. His most famous yacht was the brig *Waterwitch* with which, in 1833, he challenged Mr. C. H. M. Talbot to a race from the Nab round the Eddystone lighthouse and back (about 224 miles). Mr. Talbot's vessel was *Galatea,* a schooner. *Waterwitch,* a vessel of exceptional speed, won by 25 minutes. With her Lord Belfast frequently took on warships leaving Portsmouth harbour in impromptu speed trials and outsailed them so frequently than in 1834 the Admiralty bought *Waterwitch* for use as a trial horse with ships of the fleet.

The initiative of that other remarkable yachtsman, Mr. Assheton-Smith, in commissioning the first steam yacht in 1830 was not to bear such immediate fruit. Steam yachts continued to be objects of abuse. However, the prejudice against them was partially overcome by the commissioning of one by Queen Victoria as her first Royal yacht. This action went far to set the stamp of respectability upon hitherto unmentionable machinery.

1838 TO 1919

The Victorian Era and its Clubs

'To be an Englishman is to belong to the most exclusive Club there is.'
Ogden Nash

*I*n Queen Victoria, Britain had once again a sovereign who was interested in yachts. She did not expect a yacht to be a floating pavilion but a ship with, to some extent, a ship's way of life. The first *Victoria and Albert* was launched in 1843. In 1856 (and after a second *Victoria and Albert* had been launched in the previous year), the Royal Yacht Squadron permitted its members to become owners of steam yachts.

The Victorian era was the era of yacht clubs. The Royal Thames and the Royal Northern Yacht Clubs had both been established in pre-Victorian days but it was after 1838 that the concept of the yacht club really took hold and spread. On coming to the throne Queen Victoria became patroness of the Royal Thames Yacht Club. This club, the oldest of the English yacht clubs, had grown steadily. Some hard feeling (and words) resulted from the removal by the Admiralty of the right of flying the coveted White Ensign from the club (and incidentally from a number of other clubs too) leaving only the Royal Yacht Squadron with the privilege. The Royal London Yacht Club (established in 1833) was one of the first clubs to be founded in Queen Victoria's reign. The Club, whose headquarters is now at Cowes, Isle of Wight, was originally of Metropolitan origin, at one time being housed at the Caledonian Hotel, Adelphi. Also in 1838 was founded the Royal Hobart Regatta Association. It was in this year that the first real regatta was held in Tasmanian waters, although there are records of races between vessels in these waters as early as 1831. (There is often misconception over the word 'Regatta', a Venetian word originally applying to rowing boats, not sail, but which through usage has come to signify the latter.) In 1838 also was founded the Royal Southern Yacht Club, originally at Southampton, but now quartered at Hamble on the river of that name. The Royal Harwich Yacht Club was founded in 1843 and the Royal Mersey in the following year. Also in 1844 was founded the Royal Bermuda Yacht Club, whose chronicles refer to 'the first International yacht race ever sailed' which took place on 8 May 1849 between the Bermuda yacht *Pearl* and the American *Brenda*; *Pearl* winning by the small margin of 55 seconds. Here too, is recorded the first Ocean race from the United States to Bermuda in 1906; three yachts competing under the auspices of the Brooklyn Yacht Club and the Royal Bermuda for a cup presented by Sir Thomas Lipton.

Measurement Rules

*C*lubs fulfil both a social function and a rule-making function. In the early days of Victorian yachting however there were considerable discrepancies in the conditions and rules under which yachts raced. In fact there were no fixed rules. A Victorian yachtsman or club would issue a challenge producing their own rules, rules which unquestionably favoured their own vessel or vessels. The challenged yachtsman or club would then reply with an acceptance of the challenge provided that their own rules were adopted. These would be enclosed with the acceptance and naturally were designed to favour the challenged. So the race was fought on paper to start with until some compromise was reached over the rules.

Although there was plenty of organized yacht racing in the early nineteenth century, the obvious fact that a yacht's potential speed is related to her length was not taken into serious consideration. Consequently races were open to all comers; there were no classifications and no time allowances. Obviously under such conditions, no matter who started the race, it soon resolved itself into a contest between a small number of the larger and faster craft. As we have seen, the Royal Yacht Squadron had attempted in 1829 to do something about this with their 'six classes' handicap rule. But a more sophisticated system was needed, and a more sophisticated formula for measuring the yachts. A measurement formula had been in force since 1694. This dealt with tonnage.

pages 24 and 25:
The first Victoria and Albert. *The Royal Steam Yacht is shown at Spithead on 28 August 1843 in a painting by H. John Vernon. Also in the picture are the R.Y.S. yacht* Kestrel *and H.M.S.* Vincent *with her yards manned in the Queen's honour.*

Cutter yacht Pearl *belonging to the Marquess of Anglesey. (She was launched in 1821.)*

This formula was:

$$\frac{Length \times beam \times depth\ of\ hold}{100}$$

The length measurement was along the keel.

A modification of this, known as the 'Builders' Measurement' had been produced in 1770. Yachtsmen in the early nineteenth century, looking for some yardstick by which to measure their craft, adopted the Builders' Measurement system. Since those who were building new yachts could cheat the rule by evading the keel length Builders' Measurement, some clubs varied the way in which this length measurement was determined. Principal among them was the Royal Thames Yacht Club and in their modification (in 1855), the influence of a measurement rule upon the form of a yacht's hull can be seen for the first time.

The attitude of most racing yachtsmen to the control of yacht design was simple and uniform. Their common object was speed. However, in 1851 an event occurred in the yachting world which was to upset the complacency of British yachtsmen. That something was the victory in a race of the schooner *America*.

Clean, sweet lines of the schooner
America.

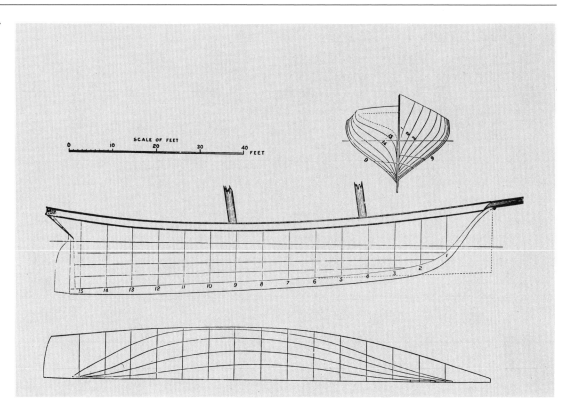

John C. Stevens.

John Stevens' American schooner
Gimcrack, *whose saloon saw the*
birth of the New York Yacht Club.

Cleopatra's Barge, *George Crown-inshield's brigantine. This famous vessel is reputed to have cost fifty thousand dollars. Below decks she was lavishly furnished in mahogany and bird's-eye maple.*

Captain George Crowninshield.

pages 28 and 29:
Schooner yacht Wyvern *(205 tons), in trouble. Her main mast carried away in a match for H.R.H. Prince Albert's Cup at Cowes, 21 August 1848, with the Earl of Cardigan's yacht* Enchantress *off the Nab Light. Painted by N. M. Condy.*

Early American Yachting

'America is a country
of young men.'
Ralph Waldo Emerson

Yachting in the United States of America may be said to have begun in the seventeenth century with the Dutch settlers in that country. In 1664 New York was occupied by the British but most of the Dutch settlers continued to live there. It could be argued, therefore, that the Dutch Americans had yachts before the British. But this lies in the realm of conjecture.

Visual proof that yachting existed in America in 1717 is shown in an engraving of New York Harbour published by William Burgess. Several yachts are seen, and an index states that one of these is 'Colonel Morris' *Fancy* turning to windward with a sloop of common mould'. A paragraph in the memorial history of New York says 'racing on the water was not much in fashion, though the gentry had their barges, and some their yachts or pleasure boats . . .' But it is in the early nineteenth century that the history of American yachting really begins and it begins with two remarkable families: the family of Stevens and the family of Crowninshield. The Stevens brothers lived in Hoboken. Crossing the Hudson river from New York to Hoboken by the ferry boat was slow and irregular. The Stevens brothers had each a boat of his own and through ferrying themselves across the river by both oar and sail they became expert at manoeuvring small craft. The first boat of John C. Stevens was the *Diver*, built in 1809. Little is known about her for there is in existence no record save the fact that she was 23 foot long. However, in 1816 Stevens built a vessel called *Trouble*. She was a larger craft, 56 foot long; two-masted, one in the extreme bow and the other a little aft of mid-ships. She had a round, full bow and was wide and flat-bottomed; a style of vessel popular in those times called a pirogue. In 1820 Stevens built a twin-hulled boat, a Catamaran named *Double Trouble*. In 1832 he built a schooner, *Wave*; 65 foot on the load-water line. *Wave* was undoubtedly a very fast vessel, for records show that in 1835, and in the subsequent year, she visited Boston and soundly defeated all the local yachts. One of the most famous of John Stevens' yachts was *Gimcrack*; a schooner built in 1844 at Hoboken. Her designer George Steers was to become famous as the designer among other notable vessels of the schooner *America*. One of *Gimcrack*'s claims to fame is that her saloon saw the birth of the New York Yacht Club. This is recorded in the first minutes of the club on board of *Gimcrack* '. . . off the Battery (New York Harbour) July 30 1844 5.30 pm', it was signed 'John C. Jay Recording Secretary'.

Formation of the New York Yacht Club was coincidental with, rather than productive of, a widening interest in yachting. Many new vessels were built including Commodore Stevens' most famous yacht *Maria*, designed again by George Steers and built by William Capes of Hoboken. When Stevens died *Maria* became the property of his brother Edward who altered her rig to that

of a schooner (she was originally rigged as a sloop). She was eventually sold and used in the fruit trade and finally met her end in a storm off Hatteras in 1870.

The other family associated with the early days of American yachting was Crowninshield. During the 1812 War the Crowninshields had run a shipping business in Salem, Massachusetts. It was an open secret that they engaged in privateering. By capturing British ships and selling both them and the cargo they made a fortune of over a million dollars. One of the products of this fortune was a yacht called

Cleopatra's Barge. This 100-foot-long vessel was built at Becket's shipyard in Salem. She was brigantine-rigged. Her cost is reputed to be fifty thousand dollars. In 1817 George Crowninshield made a highly successful Mediterranean cruise in *Cleopatra's Barge*. Stories of this cruise have passed into legend, including that of some Italians who, visiting the ship, were so impressed by the carving of an American Indian in full war paint on deck that they kissed its feet in the belief that it was an American Saint. Crowninshield planned a second voyage to England but died before he could set sail. Like *Maria*, *Cleopatra's*

Barge suffered an eventual decline in fortune, ending in the seemingly inevitable wreck. After a varied career in commerce, she ended her life on a Polynesian reef under the command of her owner, King Kanenhaneha II of the Sandwich Islands.

Of these two pioneers of American yachting, it is the Stevens family which was involved particularly with the victory over English yachts in their own waters of the schooner *America*. The 'one hundred guinea cup', which constituted the prize for this race in 1851, has ever since been known as the *America's* Cup. Twenty attempts

The schooner America. *Note pronounced rake of masts.*

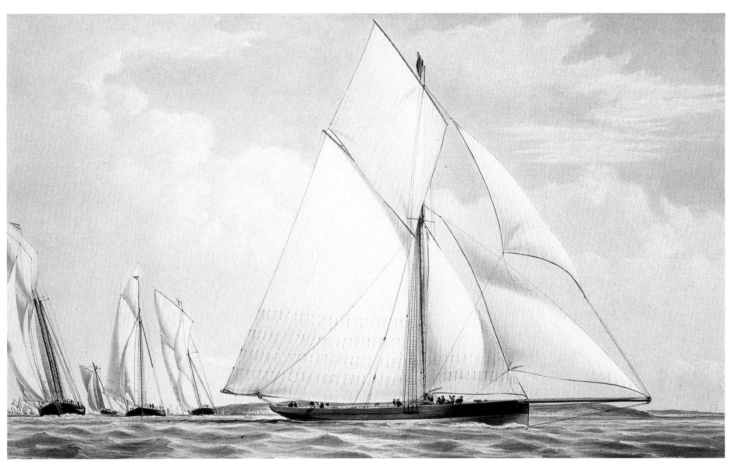

above:
Julia, *110-ton cutter, racing off the No Man buoy in a match for the R.Y.S. Cup, 9 August 1853.* Arrow, Sylvia *and* Aurora *are shown astern on the right.*

above left:
Schooner yacht Alarm *(248 tons). Rigged as a cutter of 193 tons she won several races between 1830 and 1851. In 1852 she was lengthened by the bow 20 feet and rigged as a schooner.*

left:
Schooner yacht Wyvern *passing under Clifton suspension bridge (by N. M. Condy).*

right:
Maria *a well-known American centre-board sloop raced as a trial horse against* America *in 1851— and beat her!*

**The Schooner *America*
and Her Cup Race**

have been made in vain to win this cup back from the Americans. The fact that no one has been able to do so and the enormous expense involved has given the race a special prestige.

America was owned by a syndicate of Americans headed by Commodore John C. Stevens. There had been an exchange of letters in February and March 1851 between John C. Stevens and Lord Wilton, Commodore of the Royal Yacht Squadron. The letter was in fact little more than an invitation to Commodore Stevens and his crew to become visitors of the Club House at Cowes during their stay in England. The schooner *America* crossed the Atlantic and was refitted at Le Havre. She then crossed the Channel and came to anchor off Cowes. The story goes that off the Needles a British cutter, *Laverock*, engaged her in an impromptu race. In this race *Laverock* was soundly defeated. This clearly made an impression. For several weeks no English yacht seemed prepared to offer the *America* a race. Eventually the Royal Yacht Squadron invited her to a race with fourteen British yachts round the Isle of Wight for a hundred guinea cup.

There are innumerable accounts of this race. *America*, sailing in waters of which she had no local knowledge of tides and counter currents, decisively defeated the best yachts that the Royal Yacht Squadron could produce. This victory caused a lot of analyzing and rethinking on the part of British designers. British yachts of those days were of heavy displacement, narrow beam and with very deep keels. *America* (designed by George Steers and built at William Brown's New York shipyard) was 101 feet 9 inches long, 90 feet 3 inches on the load-water-line. She had a beam of 23 feet and a draft of 11 feet. By comparison with the British vessels her draft was relatively shallow and she was a good deal broader. But it did not end there. Some of the most revolutionary things about her were the cut, material and texture of her sails. At this time, British sails were cut from loose-texture handwoven flax. They were cut full and were loose-footed. By contrast, *America*'s sails were made of close-texture, machine-woven cotton. Her two masts were raked sharply aft and from them she could set over 5,000 square feet of sail. Both her main and fore-sails were laced to the booms and not loose-footed.

The fleet who challenged the *America* was made up as follows: *Beatrice*, 161 tons; the big schooner *Brilliant*, 392 tons; *Alarm*, 193 tons; *Arrow,* 184 tons; *Volante*, 48 tons; *Wyvern*, 205 tons; *Ione*, 75 tons; *Gypsy Queen*, 160 tons; *Constance*, 218 tons; *Bacchante*, 80 tons; *Freak*, 60 tons; *Eclipse*, 60 tons and *Aurora,* 47 tons. At the start the vessels were moored in two lines. *America* was the last to get under way under a light variable breeze blowing from the west. It was 5.47 pm when she rounded the Needles on the last leg of the course. It took her three hours

to reach Cowes in the light air still blowing from the west. When she finally let go anchor crossing the finishing line amidst gunfire and the ringing of ship's bells, few noticed the arrival only 8 minutes later of the gallant little *Aurora*, the smallest vessel in the race and the only one who had given *America* any real competition. The British had bad luck earlier in the race. *Arrow* fouled her fellow competitor *Volante* and as a result *Arrow* ran ashore. *Alarm* stayed by in case she required assistance. This was indeed a piece of misfortune for the British since *Arrow* and *Alarm* were with *Volante* the three fastest yachts in the British fleet. But whichever way one looked at it nothing could detract from *America*'s performance and her speed. Her interesting hull form and superiority in sails set many tongues wagging and many a designer pondering. In this way the *America*'s Cup races began. The Cup was taken to the United States, given under terms embodied in a deed of gift—'To be preserved as a perpetual Challenge Cup for friendly competition between foreign countries'.

The schooner *America* like *Maria* and

A Sandbagger. Beamy, shoaldraft centre-boarders, they had 50-pound sandbags as movable ballast.

Cleopatra's Barge, had an eventful subsequent career. Amongst other things she is supposed to have taken part in the American Civil War, and, under the name *Memphis*, to have been a blockade runner. She now has her place in history; the yacht that was 'built to represent a nation'; and which started the most famous yachting contest of all time.

It was appropriate that the *America* should have been a schooner, for the schooner rig has always been popular in the U.S.A. The first schooner is said to have been built at Gloucester, Massachusetts in 1713. She was a work-boat and she is mentioned in Babson's *History of Gloucester*. Another typically American vessel is the sandbagger, so called because sandbags were used as ballast. Sandbaggers were descended from the watermen of New York's half-deckers and began to be raced regularly in the 1850s. The single-masted 'cat' boat with no headsail is another typical American product. But of all such, it is the schooner which takes the prize for beauty, and sometimes, as with the *America*, for performance, as well.

**More About
Measurement Rules**

' "Not men but measures":
a sort of charm by
which many people get
loose from every
honourable
engagement.'
Edmund Burke

left:
Painting of Thistle *by Henry
Shields.*

below:
America*'s Cup race off Sandy
Hook, 30 September 1887, between
American cutter* Volunteer *(Eastern
Yacht Club) and English cutter*
Thistle *(Royal Clyde Y.C.). Ed-
ward·Burgess designed* Volunteer
and George L. Watson designed
Thistle. Volunteer *won by 11
minutes 49½ seconds. Painted by
James G. Tyler.*

The yachts of the early nineteenth century were descended, from the point of view of design, from workboats. Even the schooner *America* had been based upon a New York pilot boat. We have already seen that a rule for measuring racing yachts existed but by the middle of the nineteenth century it was unsatisfactory, for it was years out of date. The rule consisted of a time allowance scale against Builders' Measurements. It taxed beam and length of keel. It did not tax either draft or length of water-line. It is not difficult to picture the kind of yachts which the designers, in trying to get around the rule, produced. They were very narrow because beam was taxed. They were very deep because draft was not. They were very long on the water-line which was not taxed but short of keel, which was. Upon these long, narrow, deep hulls were set vast areas of canvas. Stern-posts were given a pronounced rake and forefeet were cut away to nothing. These 'tonnage-cheaters' naturally enough swept the board with the older type of yacht, but it was not because they were better boats but simply because of the advantages obtained under the rule. In 1854 both the Royal London Yacht Club and the Royal Mersey Yacht Club tried to put matters right by altering the length component of the Builders' Rule Formula. Now the rule-cheating yachts were rated much more highly; in some instances they found themselves having to give time allowance to the older vessels. The outcry which this raised in certain quarters caused the Royal Thames Yacht Club to amend the rule again, producing the 'Thames Measurement' Rule. The formula ran as follows:

$$\frac{(Length - Beam) \times Beam \times \frac{1}{2}\,Beam}{94}$$

This well-known formula has persisted to this day in so far as it is used to describe a given size of yacht, particularly a cruising yacht. One still sees '5 tonner', '8 tonner' in yachting advertisements, although the practice is now dying out and other more up-to-date descriptions (like I.O.R. Rating) are used. However, the effect on yacht design of this formula from 1855 onwards was by no means satisfactory. The rule penalized beam, so yachts got steadily narrower. Sail area, not being taxed, grew and grew. Bowsprits were long and so were counters, with rudder-posts well inboard (giving untaxed waterline length when heeled). These extreme creations were known as 'plank-on-edge' yachts.

**Formation of the
Yacht Racing Association**

*M*any new yachts were built under the new Thames Measurement Rule. In this spate of activity some significant innovations were made. In 1874 William Froude published a work on the frictional resistance of water. The following year, an agricultural implement maker named Bentall designed his own boat *Jullanar*. The novel ideas embodied in *Jullanar* created a sensation but in 1877 the designer G. L. Watson went much further and produced *Thistle*, a development of *Jullanar*, a vessel so cut away that even the designer came to the conclusion that he had overdone it. *Thistle* raced for the *America*'s Cup but was easily beaten by the American yacht *Volunteer*.

Jullanar and *Thistle* were called brilliant, inventive designs by some, but 'rule-cheaters' by many more. Designers were becoming too clever for the rule-makers and in 1875 a group of yachtsmen realizing that something must be done formed the Yacht Racing Association. The Association made a number of attempts to come to grips with the matter. In 1881 welcome

The British Royal cutter Britannia.

Navahoe *(right) and the 23-metre* Nyria *in a tacking duel.*

authority and prestige came to the Association when the Prince of Wales became President. It was time something was done. In spite of the efforts of the rule-makers yachts continued to get narrower and crankier, culminating in the famous *Oona* which had an overall length of 46 feet, a waterline length of 32 feet and draft of 8 feet and a beam of only 5 feet 6 inches! She was wrecked off the Irish coast.

Fortunately somebody appeared on the scene with an answer. In 1886 comparative measurement in terms of tons was abolished and the tax on beam and dimensions removed. The new criterion was compounded of the speed factors of water-line length and sail area multiplied together and divided by a denominator of 6,000; this produced a rating figure. This rule was produced by a designer of considerable ability, by name Dixon-Kemp, who published in 1876 a classic work on the subject. But Dixon-Kemp's rule, and others which followed it, were inadequate in some respects. The problem was not effectively dealt with until the international

conference of 1906; an event described in a subsequent chapter; but the word 'international' emphasizes that yachting by this time was by no means a British-American monopoly.

For the rapidly expanding and developing sport of yachting, the last half of the nineteenth century is of great significance. It is erroneous to assume that yachting and yacht racing developed in England and the British Colonies and the United States of America alone. By the mid-nineteenth century it had spread to or developed in many other countries. Organized yachting in a country may be assumed to be well established with the existence of one or more large clubs. Mention of one or two of these therefore, can be taken as representative of the whole. Early starters in the race were the French. The first French regatta was held at Dieppe on 12 August 1837; a similar regatta took place at Le Havre on 18 August 1839. They were both for rowing boats. The committee which had run the Le Havre regatta organized a 'sailing' regatta in July 1840 and at the end of that year the Societé des Régates du Havre, the first yacht club in France, was formed. A committee presided over by Monsieur Mathurin Cor drew up the first tonnage rule (some fifteen years before the Thames Measurement rule). The well-known Yacht Club de France was first mooted by the Vicomte de Dreuille, owner of two yachts, *Caprice* and *Satanité,* at a meeting on 8 January 1858 of the Societé des Régates Parisienne, and the Duc de Vallondrose became its first Commodore.

Earlier in the race than the French was the first of the Nordic yacht clubs, the Segel Sällskabet, later to become the Royal Swedish Yacht Club, founded in Stockholm in 1830. The new club quickly grew in size and influence, and two years later the right to fly a royal flag was granted by King Carl Johan.

Although the word 'yacht' came from the Dutch, they were not the first in the field to organize clubs for the sport they invented; the first Dutch yacht club in Holland being founded in Rotterdam in 1846. It was called the Royal Yacht Club of the Low Countries (Koninklijke Nederlandsche Jachtclub). Prince Henry, brother of the future King William III was a founder member. Other yacht clubs followed rapidly; Amsterdam in 1847; the Maas at Rotterdam in 1851 and another at Dordrecht.

The first yacht club to be formed in Germany started life on 7 January 1855 at Koenigsberg in Eastern Prussia. Its name was Segel-Club Rhe. After East Prussia was captured by the Russians, the Club transferred to Hamburg. Kiel was to become the fashionable German sailing centre, and by the beginning of the twentieth century had developed sufficiently to rival Cowes in England. Great impetus came from the Emperor William II's enthusiasm for yachting. In 1901 he bought his first yacht *Thistle*, followed by a series

European Yacht Clubs

Anglo-American yacht race of 1870. Start of the yachts Dauntless *and* Cambria *from Queenstown for New York on 4 July.* Dauntless, *an American schooner of 321 tons owned by James Gordon Bennett, Jnr., Vice-Commodore of the New York Yacht Club, took 23 days 7 hours to complete the course. Her opponent, the English schooner* Cambria *(188 tons) owned by John Ashbury, Commodore of the Royal Harwich Yacht Club, took 23 days 17 mins. 15 seconds. Lithograph by T. G. Dutton from a painting by R. L. Stopford.*

Shamrock II *dismasted 22 May 1901. Sir Thomas Lipton's* America*'s Cup challenger's entire rig collapsed during a trial. King Edward VII, who was aboard, nonchalantly lit a cigar. The accident postponed the cup series for a month.*

of yachts called *Meteor*. The principal club in Kiel was the Kaiserlicher Yacht Club. Founded in 1887, the Emperor was Commodore.

As in England, the 1850s saw the start of many European clubs. Two Spanish clubs, the 'Real Sporting' and the 'Club del Albe' date from this time and Portugal also had its 'Real Association Naval' founded in 1856.

The early Belgian yacht clubs were all founded in the 1860s; the Royal Yacht Club d'Ostende in 1860, the Antwerp Club in 1860 and the Sailing Club de Gand in 1867; the latter changing its name in the following year to the Royal Belgian Sailing Club. Another mid-nineteenth century-founded yacht club was the Royal Danish, the principal yacht club of Denmark, which started in 1860. To begin with, yachts and work-boats raced together in an unorganized fashion. However with improvement in hull design and the increasing sail areas of the yachts the work-boats could no longer hold their own, and handicap

racing was put on a properly organized basis for the first time in 1887.

In Italy, last in chronological order of this list, yachting was first put on an organized basis at Genoa. A certain Captain Enrico d'Albertis, a former officer of the Italian Navy, who owned a yacht *Violande*, was the prime mover in starting the Yacht Club Italiano in 1879. In the following year, the King of Italy and the Princes d'Aoste and de Genes joined the club and the first regatta was held in the Gulf of La Spezia.

The details of these clubs, here limited by space, do less than justice to these (and other unmentioned) foreign yacht clubs of distinction. Such bare facts tell nothing of the pangs of birth of these organizations, or the efforts to devise rules and conditions for racing. The bleak recounting of founders' names however distinguished, does not tell the reader of the early struggles and triumphs nor help him to visualize either the clash of personalities in the long

Shamrock I *disabled. Lipton's* Shamrock I, *which unsuccessfully challenged J. Pierpoint Morgan's* Columbia, *lost her steel gaff due to over-canvassing on 13 September 1899.*

histories of these clubs, nor hear the triumphant gun that announces the winning yacht, latest in nautical design, the product of years of research.

But at least it will now be clear that the early part and middle of the nineteenth century, which witnessed the start of organized yachting and yacht racing in British and American waters, saw very much the same thing in many other countries. Many countries were, as we shall see, to join together to form the International Yacht Racing Union in 1906. By the second half of the century, yachting was practised extensively. From now on the story, though by no means identical, is similar in various parts of the world. The object of the racing yacht owner is to win the race. The object of the designer is to design a boat which will go faster than other boats. The object of the rule makers is to devise rules to promote fair sailing and to contain the enthusiasm of the designers within seamanlike bounds.

In Britain, in the last decade of the nineteenth century it was possible to see the results of the new rule of measurement devised in 1886 by Dixon-Kemp—results which on the whole were satisfactory. Although there were features of the rule that were far from ideal, some wonderful large cutters were built at this time. Of these, none was more successful than the Royal Yacht *Britannia*, designed by George Watson for the Prince of Wales. A cutter called *Navahoe* arrived from America in 1893. When the two yachts met, *Britannia* won twelve out of thirteen races. In the following year another American visitor *Vigilant*, arrived to take on *Britannia*. *Vigilant* was considered at that time to be the most advanced yacht in America; an 87-foot water-line cutter, she carried 12,330 square feet of sail. Once again *Britannia* was the victor. *Vigilant* had successfully defended the *America*'s Cup by beating Lord Dunraven's *Valkyrie II*. But in British waters she could not beat *Britannia* who won twelve of seventeen races.

America's Cup Races

Lord Dunraven. In the 1895 series Lord Dunraven (pictured here) fouled the American 'defender' in Valkyrie III. *The incident aroused much controversy.*

Crew of U.S. America's Cup yacht Defender, *which defeated Lord Dunraven's* Valkyrie III *in 1897.*

*B*ritannia may have beaten *Vigilant* but she was not competing in the *America's* Cup race. Ever since its inception British efforts to win back the trophy had met with signal failure. The first challenge in 1870 had been acrimonious. An argument as to whether the challenger should race against one defender or against a whole fleet had developed. The result was that Mr. James Ashbury's *Cambria* raced against a fleet of seventeen. Ashbury also objected to the fact that a number of the American yachts were of shallow draft with centre-boards. *Cambria* was tenth in the race. In 1871 came the second British challenge; this time with only two yachts taking part. However, the Americans claimed that if they wished they could select a different defender each day, according to weather conditions. In 1876 and 1881 the challenges came from Canada and both of them failed.

In 1885 the Americans agreed that only one yacht could be selected to defend each challenge but they stipulated that if a yacht was defeated

in a challenge she could not challenge again for two years. They also stipulated that the challenging yacht had to cross the Atlantic herself and not be shipped across, and that challenges had to be issued ten months in advance, giving the proposed dimensions of the challenger. With these three provisos the Americans secured a good deal for themselves, particularly in the last clause, for they could build potential defenders with the dimensions of the challenger known to them and then choose the best. Perhaps not surprisingly the next three challenges were unsuccessful. Then came 1893 and hope centered on *Valkyrie II* a beautiful yacht from the board of G. L. Watson, the designer of *Britannia*. *Valkyrie II* was built for the Earl of Dunraven. Lord Dunraven came nearer winning than any of his predecessors. Encouraged by this he challenged again in 1895. This was a most unfortunate series which led to accusations by Lord Dunraven. There was a hearing before a committee in America and much newspaper publicity and a great deal of ill-feeling was

'There is many a slip 'twixt the CUP and the LIP(ton)'—An American cartoon referring to Sir Thomas Lipton's second loss.

The launching of Valkyrie III.

Shamrock V, *17 June 1931.*

The German Emperor.

The launching of Shamrock IV *May 1914, with H.M.S.* Victory *in the background.*

right:
King Edward VII and King Alfonso of Spain.

engendered on both sides of the Atlantic. From the point of view of handicapping, the races for the cup until 1920 were on time allowance. The challenger, on arriving in American waters, would be measured according to the American rule and given a rating and a time allowance was applied to the distance of the course.

In 1899 came a challenge by Thomas Lipton. Sir Thomas Lipton, millionaire head of a grocery empire was to be a most determined challenger. For the 1899 series (made under the flag of the Royal Ulster Yacht Club) Lipton entered *Shamrock*, designed by William Fife. The defender was *Columbia* designed by Nat Herreshof. The two yachts were remarkably similar in design but the American yacht, well skippered by Charlie Barr, emerged the victor. Undaunted, Lipton challenged with *Shamrock II*, and this time the designer was G. L. Watson. Once again *Columbia* defended with Charlie Barr as skipper, and once again Lipton was defeated. His third challenge in 1903 with *Shamrock III* was also unsuccessful. *Reliance* designed by Nat Herreshof was undoubtedly the faster boat.

Sir Thomas Lipton tried for thirty years to win the *America's* Cup. From 1899 to 1930 he was the only challenger. He was over eighty years old when he issued his last and fifth challenge. His new yacht *Shamrock V* was the first in the 'J' Class series; her designer was Charles Nicholson. To defend, the Americans built four 'J' Class yachts and selected the Starling Burgess-designed *Enterprise*. In the 1931 series *Shamrock V* was decisively beaten. The following year Sir Thomas Lipton died but he had seen the *America's* Cup (in no small way due to his own efforts) rise to the most prestigious racing event in the world.

It had been a battle of millionaires. Beginning with Pierpont Morgan owner of the first *Columbia*, Sir Thomas had challenged in turn the following: *Reliance*, owner Cornelius Vanderbilt syndicate; *Resolute*, owner Henry Walters syndicate; *Enterprise*, owner Harold S. Vanderbilt syndicate. With the arrival of the 'J' Class the stage was now set for the challenge of T. O. M. Sopwith's *Endeavour* (in 1934) undoubtedly the finest and fastest yacht ever designed by Charles Nicholson; but this belongs to the next chapter.

King George V painted at the helm of Britannia.

Sir Thomas Lipton.

left:
The launching of Endeavour. *Sop-with's great hope—designed by Charles Nicholson—she nearly won the series.*

The American designer Nathaniel Greene Herreshof dominated the scene in both designing and building from the 1890s onwards for almost fifty years.

Mr. T. O. M. Sopwith at helm of Endeavour.

right:
Charles Barr. Renowned U.S. skipper and master helmsman.

Endeavour.

Resolute, *last of the gaff-rigged America's Cup defenders to carry mast-headers.*

Enterprise *below decks; showing completely functional interior.*

Hoisting the mainsail aboard Reliance.

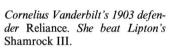

Cornelius Vanderbilt's 1903 defender Reliance. *She beat Lipton's* Shamrock III.

Steam Yachts

'Oh, where are you
going to, all you big
steamers,
With England's own
coal, up and down the
salt seas?'
Rudyard Kipling

While certain yachting millionaires on both sides of the Atlantic were engaged in trying to win or defend the *America's* Cup; others were busily occupied with another even more expensive mode of navigating the seas. They were building huge steam yachts.

In practice, the development of the steam yacht, pure and simple, was slow. In chapter II we left Mr. Assheton-Smith parting company with the Royal Yacht Squadron over a divergence of views on such vessels. Doubtless influenced partly by the fact that Queen Victoria had built two Royal steam yachts (both called *Victoria and Albert*) the Squadron in 1856 removed the embargo, but in spite of this few English steam yachts were built. What did appear were a number of large, auxiliary, sailing vessels; vessels like Lord Brassey's auxiliary steam yacht *Sunbeam* and *Czarina,* the 564-ton auxiliary schooner owned by his brother. Lord Brassey made a world cruise in *Sunbeam*, which, while in American waters, was much admired. Commodore Curtiss James, a victim of her comeliness, built an auxiliary steam yacht with the full intention of following in the footsteps of Lord Brassey's world cruise. James' yacht *Aloha*, was 180 foot long and barque-rigged. But Commodore James was the exception to the rule. American yachtsmen did not have the same antagonism to the pure steam yacht as their British counterparts and those who wanted a 'steam yacht' saw no reason why they should not have just that. In 1855 the first large American steam yacht, *North Star*, was built for Cornelius Vanderbilt I. This vessel—and others which were to follow—epitomized the multi-millionaire's luxurious yacht. Some 270 foot long, she cost over half a million dollars to build. She was built in oak by Jeremiah Symonson and was driven by two huge paddle-wheels, 34 foot in diameter.

The last half of the nineteenth century was the true era of the American multi-millionaire tycoon. Other tycoons have followed, but the original, unabashed revelling in money and lavish spending of it has never been quite the same since the two world wars. There is something irresistible about the monster vessels which these men considered to be so essential a part of their equipment. The basic requirements in so far as yachts were concerned were simple. Speed to get about the oceans, comfort to the point of luxury and, perhaps above all, size. And not just one yacht—keep on building! Jacob Lorillard spent some of his tobacco fortune on a new steam yacht each year; each one larger than the previous one.

In England the scene was very different. There may have been steam engines below decks in the large auxiliary yachts of the period but the funnels were dwarfed by towering masts. Indeed in most cases, when not in use the funnels were lowerable to complete the illusion that the vessel was a sailing ship. However, by 1910 when Commodore Curtiss James was commissioning the auxiliary steam yacht *Aloha*, the tide had begun to turn, and the out-and-out steam yacht

Auxiliary schooner yacht Sunbeam *in which Lord Brassey made many long cruises including one round the world.*

Mr. Albert Brassey's auxiliary schooner yacht Czarina.

Barque-rigged Aloha. *U.S. Commodore Curtiss James's 180-foot yacht.*

Queen Victoria aboard her third and largest yacht, Victoria & Albert III, *inspects the Fleet at Spithead, June 1867.*

Corsair III. *One of J. Pierpoint Morgan's steam yachts.*

was coming to be accepted in England. The change had been slow and it produced some interesting design features. Although they had no sails, the early steam yacht's retained many of the features of a sailing vessel. Let us take as an example *Erin,* a steam yacht belonging to Sir Thomas Lipton. She had a clipper bow, long bowsprit, two masts, raked aft (almost like the schooner *America*) upon which were set staysails and a fore-sail and mizzen-sail. She had a long, gilded counter-stern. Her funnel raked back at the same angle as her masts. She represented a compromise. Although a steam yacht, she made one think of a sailing vessel. She had a definite beauty moreover, and there were many others like her.

Curiously enough these nostalgic features found favour with many of the rich American yacht owners. Some designers of course, discarded the long overhangs and produced straight-stemmed, functional-looking yachts, rather like miniature passenger liners. But there were many in America with whom the traditional drawn-out counter and bow found favour. Once the steam yacht had come to be accepted in England its development was rapid and the fleet grew and grew. The business tycoons of the late Victorian and Edwardian era were to build a fleet of steam yachts almost as impressive as that of the Americans. These vessels were not only expensive to build, they cost a fortune to run; for example, Sir Thomas Lipton's *Erin* is said to have cost £50,000 a year (which, in the period before the First World War, was a very great deal of money). It was probably about this time that the story grew of one millionaire who asked

Cornelius Vanderbilt.

Yacht Racing—'Raters' and 'One-Designs'

The German Emperor's Hohenzollern.

Sir Thomas Lipton's steam yacht Erin.

another: 'What does it cost to run a yacht?' and received the reply 'You cannot afford one. No one can afford a yacht if he has to ask what it costs!'

The steam yacht had indeed become what it had been in America for upwards of fifty years—a status symbol. But it was by no means only tycoons who engaged in the race for bigger and better steam yachts. Queen Victoria herself, complaining that the old *Victoria and Albert II* was far too small for her when compared with the Czar of Russia's *Standart* or the German Emperor's *Hohenzollern,* launched *Victoria and Albert III* in 1901. With her 5,005 tons the new Royal yacht came proudly at the top of the list in Lloyd's Register of Yachts. She was built of steel, sheathed with wood. Although undoubtedly impressive from the point of view of sheer bulk, this great vessel, with a stern which seems too truncated, masts which seem oddly placed (though pleasantly raked aft) and two funnels which seem too close together, could not be called a beautiful ship.

But if there were those—and there were plenty it seems—who could afford these luxurious vessels, in the world of yacht racing under sail the scene was changing. By the last decade of the nineteenth century racing in large yachts had come to be considered by many, who hitherto had not even thought about it, as needlessly expensive. Among other items, wages of yacht hands had risen. A cutter of 120 tons, for example, would require a crew of 25 men so that there was a sizeable annual bill for wages alone. And since it was possible, under the new Dixon-Kemp rating rules, to build smaller and cheaper boats (that is to say, cheaper to build and certainly cheaper to run), many availed themselves of this opportunity. But this trend did more than save the pockets of those who had formerly owned larger craft, it opened up the field to a new public. Men of comparatively modest means could now enjoy the fashionable sport of yacht racing.

Many classes of these 'Raters', as they were known, sprang up around the coast. They were basically half, one, two-and-a-half, and five-raters. Based on waterline length and sail area, the Dixon-Kemp calculation was simple; for example: 200 foot of sail area multiplied by 15 foot of waterline, making 3,000; divided by 6,000 and you have a 'half-rater'. These were very much smaller vessels than those they were tending to replace. Not only were they economical to build and run, they took up much less anchorage or mooring room in harbours, estuaries, etc. Of course the 'Raters' did not stop at five. There were twenty-raters, thirty-raters and so on. But it was the smaller boats that marked the significant change in the sport, which was to pave the way for the enormous fleets of small, racing class boats which were to come. In 1895 the Seawanhaka Corinthian Yacht Club of

America (Oyster Bay) gave a challenge trophy for races between British and American small rater yachts. The first race in the series, which later became known as the Seawanhaka Cup, was between the British half-rater *Spruce IV* and *Ethelwynn* which was the American equivalent of a half-rater. The American formula known as the Seawanhaka Rule produced a similar result to the British linear rating, but instead of speaking of a half-rater, the Americans referred to a 'fifteen-footer'.

In 1903 there appeared in Britain the South Coast One Design. These were by no means small boats since they measured some 73 feet overall. They were not 'Raters' exactly but they were indirectly a product of the new rating rule. What was new about them was the idea of being 'one-design'. Sailing people today are so familiar with one-design classes (indeed they outnumber the restricted or development and formula classes considerably) that it is curious to reflect that when they first appeared the idea was very unpopular with yachtsmen. A yacht was held to be individual. The idea that your boat resembled another almost exactly, or vice-versa, was as repellent to the average yacht-owner as is the sight to a woman at a smart gathering of another woman in identical dress. The idea came from the United States. By the turn of the century, classes had been established by the New York Yacht Club and there, probably because American yachtsmen were less conservative, the 'one-design' idea caught on and its advantages were soon appreciated. The advantage is not only cheapness. Part of the attraction lies in the fact that since the boats are identical, a race must be won by the skill of helmsmen and crew alone. But undoubtedly the economic factor added to the popularity of the one-designs.

In addition to the service it had rendered to the relatively impecunious yachtsman, the Dixon-Kemp linear rule of multiplying the waterline length by the sail area and dividing the result by 6,000 had produced in the last decade of the nineteenth century some magnificent ships; the two best probably being *Satanita* designed by J. M. Soper and George Watson's *Britannia*. But as the century drew to its close there were launched some very curious craft indeed. The Dixon-Kemp rule did not control the designers for long. Since length was measured along the waterline, overhangs grew, beam increased and displacement was reduced to the minimum. Keels were constructed of the 'fin and bulb' variety. With their exaggeratedly shallow hulls these boats were known as 'skimming dishes'. To check these trends the Yacht Racing Association in 1896 and in 1901 drew up their own brand of linear rules. These were based on the proposals of a naval architect by the name of R. E. Froude. These rules added to the old equation based on length and sail area, breadth and also girth, of the hull. Froude's rule did not succeed in controlling the 'skimming dishes', the girth measurement being insufficient for this purpose. So people continued to search for a rule, and as we have already noted, by now the problem was an international one.

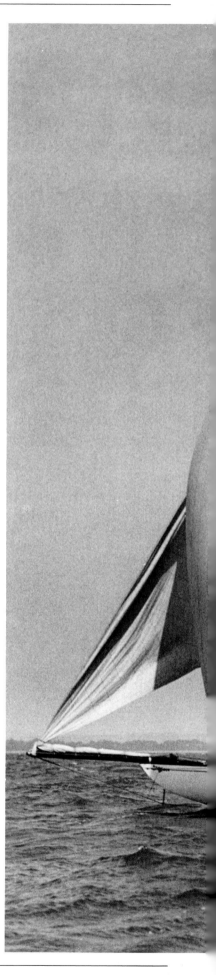

Witch, *a half-rater.*

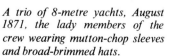

A trio of 8-metre yachts, August 1871, the lady members of the crew wearing mutton-chop sleeves and broad-brimmed hats.

Yachts of the 12-metre fleet.

15-metre yachts. (The King of Spain's Hispania *is leeward boat in the centre.)*

Taken off Cowes in 1930, this picture shows Candida *leading* Cambria, Astra *(having trouble with her spinnaker) and* Westward.

significant advance in the control and development of rating rules was to come from a meeting of European nations, who in 1906 formed the International Yacht Racing Union. The I.Y.R.U. rule continued time allowances but these were only used in the larger classes. The main body of the yacht racing classes were to race level at a rating to be named in metres. The new classes were accordingly known as 'Metre' classes. Thirteen European countries used the rule between its inception in 1907 and 1914 (the outbreak of the First World War). The classes were: 5 metres, 6 metres, 7 metres, 8 metres, 9 metres, 10 metres, 12 metres, 15 metres, 19 metres and 23 metres. They did not all survive the test of time; the 6, 8, and 12 metres being the only ones to survive the war in any significant numbers. The Americans had, in 1904, adopted their own (known as the 'Universal') rule which was devised by Nathaniel Herreshof (who had designed the successful [if rather extreme] *America*'s Cup defender *Reliance*). American yachts built under the Universal Rule were rated alphabetically. When the Europeans drew up the so-called 'International' Rule in 1906, the Americans did not elect to come within its jurisdiction and continued to race under their 'Universal' Rule.

The 'Metre' boats were to have a long run. Today they are virtually obsolete, apart from the 12 metres (*America*'s Cup); the cruiser-racer 8 metres; and a small number of isolated 6 metres around the world. And there are many, who, despite arguments of cost inflation and other relevant factors, mourn their passing.

In their heyday, in the period before World War I, they flourished as classes had never flourished before. Throughout their career they inspired the best international designers.

he last half of the nineteenth century, beginning with the victory of the schooner *America*, had witnessed a remarkable development and expansion in yacht racing. The same half of the century also saw the emergence of a type of enterprise which now seems to be almost commonplace; that is the making of long, single-handed cruises in small yachts. The first ship to cross the Atlantic under sail was a somewhat eccentric vessel called *Red White and Blue*. She was a lifeboat 26 feet in length, built of iron, with watertight compartments for buoyancy. She bore the legend 'Ingersolls Improved Metallic Lifeboat' along her sides and was rigged as a full-rigged ship. In this odd craft her American skipper William Hudson set sail on 9 July 1866. He arrived off Portland Bill on 14 August, anchoring off Deal on the following day. The vessel was exhibited in Paris and London and attracted considerable attention. The log of the voyage was published in *Hunt's Yachting Magazine* of 1866. A crossing in a more normally found vessel—albeit small—was made in 1876 when a young 'Banks' fisherman, Alfred Johnson,

The 'I.Y.R.U.' and the 'Metre' Classes

The Cult of the 'Single-Hander'

'All we ask is to be let alone.'
Jefferson Davis in 1861

German-manned and under German command, Meteor IV, *Kaiser Wilhelm II's beautiful 400-ton schooner. For his attempts to intrude successfully into the great yachting scene, dominated at the time by Anglo-American rivalry, the Emperor's previous yachts had been crewed by British sailors under British Command.*

*Norman had first made the West-East crossing in the previous year.

crossed the Atlantic single-handed in a gaff-cutter only 20 foot long. Her name was *Centenniel*. Johnson had a rough passage, being turned bottom up by a rogue sea. He was able to right the yacht, bale out and carry on. In 1877 Captain Thomas Crapo crossed the Atlantic in the 19 foot two-master *New Bedford*. In 1878 a small vessel, the *Nautilus*, made the passage, sailed by William Andrews and his brother. Andrews like Crapo, Johnson and the others was an American, and his book *A Daring Voyage Across the Atlantic* (published by Griffiths and Sarran in 1880) is well worth reading (i.e. if you can find it in a library—it is a rare yachting treasure and those who have a copy seldom care to lend it!).

Although a number of other voyages were made at this time, there is no doubt that the best-known of the American pioneer cruising men is Captain Joshua Slocum. Slocum's ship was the *Spray*. She was rebuilt from the hulk of an old sloop which he was given as a present and which he found 'propped up' in a field. He spent 1893 completely rebuilding the craft and the *Spray* was launched the following year. In 1895, at the age of 51, he sailed from Boston on his remarkable voyage round the world. The book which he wrote about it, called *Sailing Alone Around the World*, is a classic. He wrote with the economy of language and clarity of a man long accustomed to entering up a ship's log. His writing carries the same authority founded on long experience of the sea that is so manifest in the deceptively simple way he took his ship single-handed through every kind of adverse circumstance. Reprints of his book (including his voyage of the *Liberdade*) are easily obtainable.

In 1902 another American yacht *Seabird* crossed the Atlantic. She was owned and sailed by Thomas Fleming Day, editor of the American yachting magazine *Rudder*. Subsequently an account of the voyage was published under the title *Across the Atlantic in Seabird*. It is written with zest and a considerable sense of humour.

The sea passages so far mentioned have been from the New World to the Old. In 1870, an American, John Buckley, made the first east-west crossing with a friend as crew in a converted ship's lifeboat, *City of Ragusa*. The first recorded British crossing in a small vessel from east to west is that of Frederick Norman. Norman built himself a small boat, 16 foot long; rigged her as a cutter, named her *Little Western*, and created a record by being the smallest vessel to cross the Atlantic from east to west, sailing (with a friend as crew) from London in June 1881*.

Another remarkable seaman who voyaged the ocean in small boats was Captain John C. Voss. He is best known for his voyage in the 'dug-out' Indian canoe *Tilikum*. He sailed from Vancouver in 1901. When he eventually reached England, after having sailed 40,000 miles round the world, he anchored off Margate. He was asked from which port he had sailed. 'Vancouver' came the answer. 'How long on your voyage?' 'Three

years, three months' came the reply, and '. . . a loud applause followed'. Voss was another sailorman happily gifted with the ability to put his adventures on paper. Like Slocum he communicates enthusiasm and a salty humour. It must not be thought, however, that these early cruises were always of such length. Some of the most influential voyages were modest by comparison. Two British yachtsmen who were to show how cruises can be made either single-handed or with crew, in small boats and quite inexpensively, were E. F. Knight and R. T. McMullen. Edward Knight was born in 1852, son of an old soldier who had fought through the Carlist war on the staff of the Spanish Legion. He grew up to be a pioneer of yacht cruising and a sailing author of merit, best known for his three major accounts of cruises made in three different boats. Knight spoke (and speaks today—for his words have modern relevance) for those who are dismayed by the steadily mounting cost, not only of new boats, but second-hand craft as well, as inflation pushes up the prices. For such people, converted ship's lifeboats and converted fishing boats provide the answer; vessels without pretension to 'yachty' appearance but which can move from port to port and in which the owner and his friends can spend an ecstatic holiday. The other pioneer, Richard Turrel McMullen was at first sight a less prepossessing person. A Victorian stockbroker, McMullen sailed as a relaxation from his work, but his approach was anything but relaxing. Of short stature, he had intimidating energy and was a 'martinet at sea'. Of him it was written that '. . . everything had to be done as perfectly as possible, irrespective of bad weather or previous fatigue'. Knight showed what could be done for very little money in the way of cruising, but it was McMullen who proved that the single-handed amateur yachtsman could be just as efficient as a professional sailor, something no-one believed possible at the time. He raised the standard of seamanship in amateur sailing to a far higher level than had been reached before. He wrote about his voyages with surprising humour in his book *Down Channel*. One of the yachts in which he cruised, the *Leo*, built at Rotherhithe, was only three tons and only twenty foot long overall; a tiny cruising yacht for those times. Between 1850 and 1857 the martinet stockbroker sailed 8,222 miles up and down the English Channel. While Knight crossed the North Sea to the Baltic and other places, McMullen tended to stay in the Channel. He was a true pioneer of cruising yachting, having no interest in anything but cruising. When he died the *Field* said in his obituary '. . . Mr. McMullen was unlike any other yachtsman we ever met; we have known men just as fond of the sea as he was, but never anyone who regarded it with such reverential interest. Yachting and yacht racing in the ordinary sense of the terms had no charms for him'.

Another Victorian voyager to the Baltic was

Captain Joshua Slocum and (right) his yacht Spray.

American yacht Vim *in trouble with her spinnaker.*

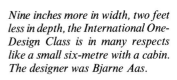

American 6-metre Goose.

Nine inches more in width, two feet less in depth, the International One-Design Class is in many respects like a small six-metre with a cabin. The designer was Bjarne Aas.

Perhaps the most famous of all racing schooners, Mr. F. T. B. Davies' 338-ton schooner, West-ward. *Built in 1910 by Nathaniel Herroshof at his yard at Bristol, Rhode Island, she was eventually enlisted for the German Emperor's maritime aspirations under the name* Hamburg II.

the Reverend Hughes. Hughes is best known for his book published in 1856 called *Two Cruises With the Baltic Fleet* which are really the log of his 8-ton yacht *Pet* in which he made two voyages to the Baltic and back. Hughes like McMullen, taught good seamanship in his writings, and both showed that a small craft properly handled was as safe in the open sea in bad weather as a large one, and furthermore that it was often safer to stay at sea in a gale of wind rather than to try and enter a harbour. Another late nineteenth century pioneer of cruising was Frank Cowper. This single-hander who was known as 'Jack-all-alone' cruised, in presumably self-imposed solitude, up and down the English Channel in a 20-foot Itchen Ferry cutter.

By the 1880's there was sufficient interest in cruising (as distinct from yacht racing) for a number of enthusiasts to meet at the chambers in Lincoln's Inn of a lawyer called Sir Arthur

Underhill, where they founded the Cruising Club (later to be honoured with the prefix 'Royal'). In 1893 the Club decided to publish charts for private circulation among its members and it has been rendering services of various kinds to cruising yachtsmen ever since. Two other clubs concerning themselves only with cruising were formed later in the century in 1908: the Cruising Association and the Clyde Cruising Club.

In their 'do-it-yourself' approach to cruising, people like Knight and McMullen were rare enough to be considered eccentrics in their day. There were some wide divergencies in people's concept of what was meant by 'cruising', and there certainly was a deal of difference between the 20-foot-long single-hander *Leo* and Lord Brassey's three-masted, auxiliary steam yacht with a crew of thirty-two and eight passengers, including the owner and his wife.

1919 TO 1939

The Bermudian Rig

With the First World War, European yachting came to a stop. However, it continued in the U.S.A. and during this period the Bermudian rig came to be adopted by inshore racing yachts. The Bermudian rig had been developed during the early part of the twentieth century. As opposed to the old gaff rig, which has a four-sided sail, the Bermudian sail is triangular. The fact that a triangular sail had long been used by vessels indigenous to the Bermuda Islands is said to have given the rig its name. It was often called 'Marconi' rig in the U.S.A., after the inventor of radio, since the complex staying required for the tall Bermudian mast made it look like a radio aerial. The well-known sailmaker, Thomas Ratsey, had developed a form of lugsail in the rater classes. During its development stages the gaff disappeared and a yard, virtually forming a continuation of the mast, took its place. This increased the height of the sail and the shape became almost triangular. For reasons both of doing away with excessive top weight and for simplicity, the yard which of course doubled the mast for about half its length, was to become the tall Bermudian mast.

International Competition in the Metre Classes

When class racing started up again in Europe after the war the Bermudian rig quickly became adopted for most classes. It started with the small classes and spread to the larger ones. After the First World War the Metre classes continued to be built and raced. They were still the perfect regatta yacht: racing machines; beautifully constructed and maintained shells of wood; long, slim, sharp-prowed and aristocratic. In the 8-metre, and particularly the 12-metre boats, accommodation in the form of berths, etc. below decks was laid down by the rules of the class, but such accommodation was kept to a minimum and as light as possible. Everything was sacrificed to speed to win races. In the year 1921 the Americans adopted the international measurement rules for yachts of 12 metres and under, and formed the North American Yacht Racing Union. This made class yacht racing truly international. The most popular class with the Americans to begin with was the 6-metre. A series of team races between Britain and the U.S.A. was arranged in this class and a new cup called the British American Cup was to be raced for alternatively in British and American waters. The series began in 1921 at Cowes and the British won. In 1922 the series was held at Oyster Bay and the British won again. The following two years also saw British victories and they won the cup outright. Competition was resumed for a new cup in 1928. This time the Americans won, they won the cup outright and they went on to win the third cup. They won in 1934, '36 and '38 and after the war in 1949. It seemed that the tables had been turned. It is difficult to pinpoint the reason. Perhaps the Americans had become more skilful. They certainly used more sails. They had been painstaking in their analysis of the reasons for British success both in tactics and in hull design.

American Success in 6 Metres—Tank Testing

But perhaps the secret lay in the new technique of testing hulls in tanks developed by Doctor K. S. Davidson. Olin Stephens, after laborious model testing in the Hoboken tank, produced his first masterpiece, the 6-metre *Goose*. About this time, in the 1920s, 6-metre yachts came to be used for races for another American cup—the Seawanhaka Cup. This was the original cup which dated back from the time of the old raters, so-called after the Seawanhaka Rule, which was the name for the American rating rule at that time. With this series of races the British had more success than with the British American 6-metre Cup. Even so, the designing know-how of Olin Stephens, the tank-testing techniques, the energetic training and practice resulting from thorough analysis of tactics, the new sail-handling techniques of Rod Stephens, all contributed to put America on top on balance in the 6-metre class.

The first International Rule had been limited to ten years, being due for revision in 1917. On account of the war it was not until 1919 that the International Yacht Racing Union was able to discuss the matter. It was decided to abandon the principle of standardizing the classes by a formula alone, and a new principle, laying down Restrictions and Limits with heavy penalties for exceeding them, was adopted. This new International Rule came into force on 1 January 1920. Restrictions (from which we get the term 'Restricted classes') applied to all racing yachts up to fourteen and a half metres rating. The rule was modified slightly in 1933.

Although the fashionable emphasis was on the Restricted class yachts in the period between the two world wars, the big class continued to race, sailing under handicap rules. *Britannia* had been re-rigged and raced regularly with *Westward* the schooner, the 23-metre *White Heather* and a number of other 23 metres including *Candida* and *Astra*.

The 'J' Class, and the *America's* Cup

In 1931 European yachtsmen adopted the American Universal Rule for the measurement of yachts over $14\frac{1}{2}$ metres. This led to the big class being reinforced by new yachts built for the new 'J' Class and such beautiful yachts as *Shamrock V*, *Endeavour* and *Velsheda* were to add lustre to big class racing in the last decade before the Second World War. There were two *Endeavours*, both designed by Charles Nicholson. With the first of these, T. O. M. Sopwith came nearer to winning the *America's* Cup for Britain

either before or since. *Endeavour*'s long steel hull measured 83 feet on the waterline and 130 feet overall. For the 1934 series, the American defender *Rainbow* was designed by Starling Burgess for a syndicate headed by Harold S. Vanderbilt. A huge spectator fleet turned up for the first race in the series on 15 September. Sopwith took the helm himself with a crew almost entirely amateur, due to a pay dispute with the original professional crew. The crew of *Rainbow* was formed of Scandinavian professionals, Vanderbilt himself taking the helm. The first race was unfinished, the time limit cutting it short, in point of fact when *Rainbow* was leading. It was re-sailed two days later, when *Endeavour* won by two minutes. Things looked favourable for Sopwith for he won the second

left:
Charles Nicholson at the wheel of Candida.

Mr. & Mrs. Sopwith on board Endeavour.

left:
Candida *close-hauled.*

below:
Starling Burgess talking to Harold Vanderbilt.

above:
Britannia *in her new Bermuda rig (note the double-clewed jib).*

Aboard Ranger: *Roderick Stephens, Olin Stevens, Professor Bliss, Mrs. Vanderbilt, Harold S. Vanderbilt at wheel and Arthur Krapp.*

race as well. In the third race the swift *Endeavour* again established a substantial lead, rounding the final mark six minutes ahead of *Rainbow*. The *America's* Cup was practically in Sopwith's hands. Harold Vanderbilt, certain that he had lost, handed the wheel over to Sherman Hoyt. Nobody is very clear what happened next. It is said that Sherman Hoyt's helmsmanship and clever use of *Rainbow's* new Genoa jib won the race. Sopwith, tacking to be on the safe side so as to keep himself between *Rainbow* and the line (a perfectly correct racing tactic), sailed into a calm. Sherman Hoyt thereupon bore away and crossed the winning line three minutes ahead of his rival.

In the fourth race came the dispute. *Endeavour*, lying to leeward of *Rainbow* tacked so as to avoid being overhauled. Under the rules, *Rainbow* as overtaking boat should have given way. She failed to do this and Sopwith had to bear away to prevent a collision. Relying on *Endeavour's* speed and hoping to win the race without lodging a protest he did not hoist a protest flag. It became apparent later that he could not win outright and he hoisted his protest flag before crossing the line. This was in order with English rules but the race committee declined to hear Sopwith's protest because under the New York Yacht Club rules the protest flag should have been hoisted at the time of the incident. Whether Sopwith's concentration or general attitude towards the race was changed by this; whether, as some say, his nerve had gone and whether indeed the crew's morale was affected, the fact remains that the fifth race was won by the Americans and in conditions that should have suited *Endeavour* perfectly. In this, the last race, Sherman Hoyt was again at the helm. Sopwith may have had bad luck, but Sherman Hoyt was a great tactician, a fact amply demonstrated by his handling of *Rainbow* in the final race. And so Sopwith's challenge failed. In 1937 he tried again with *Endeavour II* but was defeated easily. Charles Nicholson had made the lines of *Endeavour* available to the Americans after the 1934 contest. Their analysis of these lines and subsequent tank testing assisted the brilliant Olin Stephens in producing, with fellow designer Starling Burgess, a new defender, *Ranger*, which was far faster than Sopwith's second challenger.

The Second World War put an end to big class racing and with it, the 'J' Class, possibly the most spectacular yachts in racing history. Their like will not be seen again. Some of the hulls may still be glimpsed, serving as house-boats, nestling disconsolately amidst mud flats; forlorn reminders of a vanished pageant. After the death of King George V, *Britannia* was scuttled by his order on 10 July 1936. The vessel was hauled-out at Marvin's Yard at Cowes. As the yacht waited to be launched to go to her destruction the yard's foreman placed over her stern a garland of wild flowers. At midnight on 9 July she was towed into the English Channel, escorted by the Royal Navy, and scuttled by explosives.

Death of the Large Classes—The New Trends

*I*f the era between the world wars saw the end of the large classes, it also saw the increasingly rapid development of two new trends which were to expand enormously after the Second World War: the sport of dinghy racing and of racing off-shore or 'Ocean Racing'. From the West Country at Teignmouth and the East Coast of England at Norfolk, two regions long associated with yachting, come two early records of dinghies, way back at the end of the nineteenth century. The West Country dinghy recorded in 1889 was known as the 'West of England Conference' dinghy. The Norfolk dinghy, built to the rules of the Yare and Ure sailing club, was designed for sailing in rivers and inland waterways generally. It was no match for the Teignmouth dinghy. In a race between a 'Conference' dinghy and a Norfolk dinghy in 1911, the former proved to be overwhelmingly the fastest.

These were by no means the only dinghies racing as early as this but it is generally accepted that Frank Morgan-Giles, the naval architect and builder, produced in his Teignmouth shipyard, the best dinghies of his time. They were 14-footers with rounded sections. After the First World War a class was formed, developed from the original 'Conference' dinghy. It became enormously popular and in 1927 was awarded international status. Uffa Fox, another designer, who worked at Cowes, realizing that it would be difficult to improve on Morgan-Giles' design and having had experience with speed-boat hydroplanes, set out to design a V-section racing dinghy whose bows would lift out of the water when sailed hard off the wind and by halving the displacement sail, theoretically, twice as fast. He spent much time in developing hull lines which under sail would hydroplane over the water.

The First of the Modern Racing Dinghies

*I*n 1928 Fox was finally successful with his dinghy *Avenger*, winning fifty-two firsts, two seconds and three thirds in fifty-seven starts. In the same year, he also sailed *Avenger* on a cruise across the Channel to Le Havre and back. From 1928 to the outbreak of the Second World War Uffa Fox dominated the 14-foot dinghy class both in sailing as well as designing at first, and latterly, designing and building. The International 14-foot class bred some great helmsmen—Peter Scott, Chairman of the International Yacht Racing Union and Stuart Morris, who has won the Prince of Wales Cup for the class no less than twelve times, to name two. With fleets in Canada, America and New Zealand, the 14-foot class, although there are now many other classes of similar-sized racing dinghy, is not only the first of the modern racing dinghies, it still continues to provide a real test for helmsman and crew.

right:
Aboard the 'J' class in the 1930s. Velsheda on a broad reach.

pages 75 to 78:
Everything 'pinned in' hard! Close-hauled aboard Rainbow. Rainbow *was almost defeated by* Endeavour I *in 1934, but Sherman Hoyt and a little luck saved the day for the Americans and Sopwith went sadly home while the* America's *Cup stayed in America.*

pages 79-81
For fifteen years undisputed champion of the famous Grand Banks Schooners, Bluenose, *launched on 26 April 1921, was to become a legend. She was designed by W. J. Roue of Halifax and built at Smith and Rhuland's yard at Lunenburg of good Nova Scotian timber. In 1933 she appeared on Lake Michigan and at Chicago to represent Canada at the Century of Progress Exposition. In 1935 she crossed the Atlantic to represent her country at the Silver Jubilee of King George V and Queen Mary. In this fine photograph can be seen her dories stacked on deck, a reminder that her racing feats and ceremonial cruises in no way prevented her from earning her living on the Cod Banks, year after strenuous year.*
Her skipper, Captain Angus Walters, who had started at the age of thirteen as a cabin boy aboard another schooner, his father's, was to become almost as famous as Bluenose *herself. Like many another well-known vessel she ended her days sadly, trading in the Caribbean in spite of Walters' efforts to raise money to keep her in Nova Scotian waters. She was lost in 1946 off the coast of Haiti. But the tale has a twist in it, and a happy one at that, for in 1963 on 24 July, a new vessel,* Bluenose II, *built by the same shipyard to the same designer's plans, was launched by Captain Angus Walters. The dimensions of the original* Bluenose *were: length overall 143 feet; length waterline 112 feet; beam 27 feet; draft 15 feet; sail area 9,987 square feet. Her Thames Measurement Tonnage was 285.*

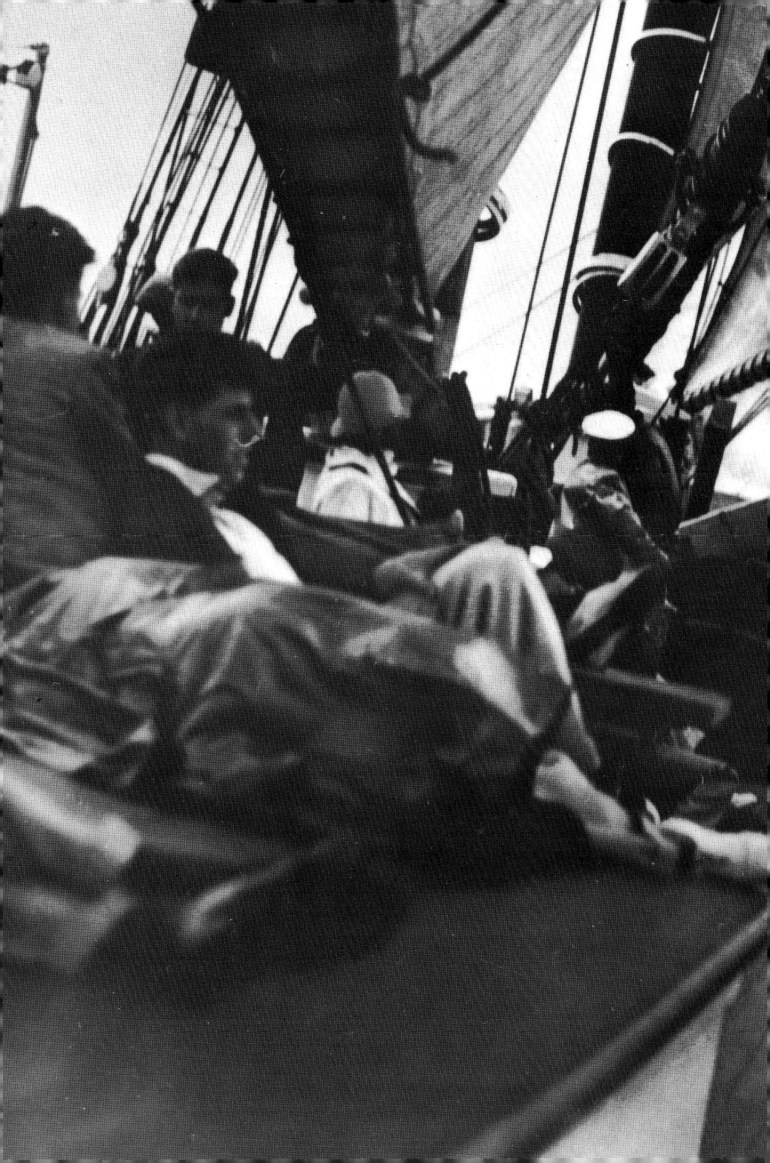

International 14-foot dinghies.

It was Uffa Fox who gave to the sliding seat canoe the title of the 'dry-fly of sailing'. The International Canoe carrying one person on a sliding seat and measuring about 17 feet is descended from the racing canoes of America. The New York Canoe Club was founded in 1871, but in the waters around New York racing in such boats is recorded as far back as 1840. The New York Canoe Club's International trophy has been raced for since 1886.

Another early dinghy, now reputed to be the most popular dinghy class in the world, the 'Snipe', just over 15 feet long, was pioneered in 1931. The American yachting magazine *Rudder* sponsored the 'Snipe'. Her designer, William Crosbie, had aimed at a hull which could be built at home cheaply. As such, the 'Snipe' had a phenomenal success. It is by no means a fast boat, especially as compared with the 14-foot

International. However, in their respective hemispheres, during the 1930s, these two boats pioneered the way for the boom in dinghy sailing which was to come after the Second World War.

The trend from small classes of large vessels to large classes of smaller boats which came to be quite apparent in the period between the wars was caused largely by economic factors. As the metre boats became slowly obsolete, other smaller keel-boat classes came to replace them. One which stands out was the International 'Dragon' designed by Norwegian Johan Anker. In the Thirties a 6-metre, a day-boat racing machine, cost about £2,000 to build. The cost of a 'Dragon' in 1930 was £240. In 1958 a 'Dragon' in Britain cost about £1,500—six times the original. Today the introduction of new building materials has helped to some extent to combat this inflation, but only 'to some extent'.

right:
Uffa Fox's first highly successful racing dinghy, Avenger.

Yachts of the enormously popular American 'Snipe' class.

Uffa Fox sailing a sliding seat canoe.

Off-Shore Racing

The between-the-wars period saw the steady growth of the new sport of off-shore racing. There had been isolated off-shore races in the nineteenth century. Three American schooners, *Henrietta, Fleetwing* and *Vesta* had raced across the Atlantic in 1866. The owner of *Henrietta* (the winner), James Gordon Bennett, took part in another well-publicized transatlantic race in 1870 in the schooner *Dauntless*. The opponent of *Dauntless* was Mr. James Ashbury's *Cambria,* another schooner. The race was from east to west. *Cambria* was in fact crossing the Atlantic anyway to challenge for the *America's* Cup. The race was won by *Cambria*. In 1887 Gordon Bennett took part in a third race with *Dauntless*, losing this time to a new schooner called *Coronet*. In 1905 the German Kaiser presented a Gold Cup for a race across the Atlantic. A three-masted fore-and-aft-rigged schooner named *Atlantic* won the Kaiser's gold cup in a record time of twelve days four hours and one minute. One hundred and eighty five foot long, this great vessel was able to maintain an average speed of over ten knots. Two of the large sailing yachts with auxiliary steam engines mentioned in Chapter IV took part in this race. They were *Sunbeam* and *Valhalla*. Their propellers had to be removed for the race, an indignity not imposed upon modern ocean racers.

Thomas Fleming Day (editor of the American magazine *Rudder*) can perhaps be called 'the daddy of ocean racing'. Like the Englishmen E. F. Knight and R. T. McMullen, Day held that a small boat was just as safe at sea as a large one, provided she was sensibly rigged and handled. In 1904 he organized a race from Brooklyn to Marble Head round Cape Cod; about 330 miles. Six small yachts crossed the line and all finished the course. Last was Day in *Seabird*. As far as Day was concerned the point had been proved but his ideas met with opposition. Ignoring this, he continued to promote them vigorously, in 1905 organizing a race from Brooklyn to Hampton Roads. Perhaps 'ignoring' is hardly the right expression, since he attacked his critics in editorials in the *Rudder* in language as salty and hard-hitting as it was well phrased. It was just the sort of controversy to send up the circulation of *Rudder* and reached a crescendo in 1906 when Day organized the first Bermuda Race. Three vessels only came to the starting line and two finished; *Tamerlane* the winner and *Gauntlet*. Also in 1906 occurred the first transpacific race from Los Angeles to Honolulu. The schooner *Lurline* was the winner. After 1906 the Bermuda race was held regularly up to the First World War. It was revived in 1923 and there was another race in the following year. In 1922 the Cruising Club of America had been founded and in the following year the members of this club, led by the influential editor of another American

magazine *Yachting*, were to be responsible for the organization of the Bermuda race.

Taking part in the Bermuda races of 1923 and 1924 was British yachtsman-author James Weston Martyr. Thanks to his efforts and those of other English enthusiasts, notably George Martin (who in the converted Havre Pilot cutter *Jolie Brise*, won the race), the first Fastnet race took place in 1925. The fleet started from Ryde in the Isle of Wight. The same year the Ocean Racing Club was founded, with George Martin as its first Commodore.

The Fastnet and the Bermuda races are the same length, 600 miles, but this is the only similarity. The first part of the Fastnet is along the south coast of England with the navigational hazards of crowded shipping lanes and fog. There are also the fast tides, races and overfalls well known to those who sail in the English Channel. After leaving Cornish waters the race then becomes more of an ocean event and heads for the Fastnet rock off the south-west corner of Ireland. The yachts then return and the finishing line is at Plymouth. The weather is as unpredictable as any English weather.

The Bermuda race is a direct course across an ocean in reasonably predictable weather; the wind often being a reaching wind, which is why from time to time schooners have done well in it. However, although it may sound simpler than the Fastnet, the east-north-easterly set of the Gulf Stream is sufficiently difficult to gauge to cause a number of yachtsmen, trying to find

Maid of Malham, designed by Jack Laurent Giles for John Illingworth, was a good example of advanced offshore design in the later 1930s. Michael Mason's fine yawl Latifa *designed and built by Camper and Nicholsons in 1936.*

The 36-ton yawl Amaryllis, *in which George Mulhauser sailed 31,000 miles round the world in the early 1920s.*

Bermuda, to have some very bad headaches indeed! (Today we have a third classic race, from Sydney to Hobart, organized by the Royal Yacht Club of Tasmania, but this did not take place until 1945 and belongs to the next chapter.) The Fastnet and the Bermuda race are biannual and are run on alternate years, the Fastnet being run as a biannual from 1929. The transpacific race has been biannual from 1926. The principal difficulty attending this race is its distance, 2,300 miles—almost four times as long as the Fastnet.

Nowadays off-shore racing tends to dominate yachting news. The modern ocean-racer, a masterpiece of functional design, fast, sea-kindly, bristling with electronic aids, is a very different vessel to the converted pilot cutter, *Jolie Brise* in which George Martin won the Fastnet way back in 1925. And yet even with that early race and the forming of the Ocean Racing Club, the essential basis of British Ocean Racing had been laid down.

Everything that was to happen in the years leading up to the outbreak of the Second World War was a natural development from the early American and British races. The Americans had got into the business sooner than the British, and it was from America that were to come many of the significant advances in the design of off-shore racing yachts. As with all forms of racing, the vexed question of rating rules came up. The two respective bodies controlling the sport in America and England, the Cruising Club of America and

left:
Colonel Baxendale's Hallowe'en, *designed by William Fife for the 1926 Fastnet, was years ahead of her time.*

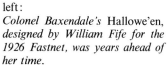

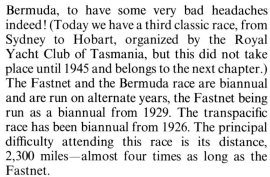

Nina, *the American yachtsman Paul Hammond's controversial and successful schooner designed by Starling Burgess. She was first of the offshore racers from America.*

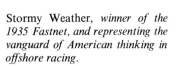

Stormy Weather, *winner of the 1935 Fastnet, and representing the vanguard of American thinking in offshore racing.*

William Albert Robinson and his Tahitian crew, Etera.

Svaap, *the ketch in which Robinson sailed around the world, passing the New York waterfront.*

the Royal Ocean Racing Club (the Club had become 'the Royal' in 1931), were, so to speak, to start together and then diverge. The Bermuda race of 1928 and a transatlantic race in 1930 were raced under British rules, but in 1932 the Cruising Club of America produced their own rules. This was a perfectly natural thing to do, of course, since the American rules could be said to be more suitable to local American conditions. The fact remains that the two rules were by this time quite different in principle. The first ocean racers were cruising boats. This made it harder to produce a rule which could give a rating from the measurements of many very different hulls and sail plans. The Royal Ocean Racing Club sought the advice of Malden Heckstall-Smith, an Englishman of great experience in such matters. The resultant rule has been a pronounced success, and with modifications lasted up to 30 September 1970, when the present International Off-shore Rule came into force, bringing English and American, and indeed international ocean-racing in line.

The early ocean racers that took part in the Fastnet were cruising yachts, gaff-rigged, heavily-sparred and of heavy displacement. However, in 1926 there appeared, specifically built for the Fastnet, a yacht called *Hallowe'en*, designed by a Scots designer, William Fife, for Colonel Baxendale. Based on a 15-metre, she had a water-line length of 50 feet. In the race her elapsed time was 3 days, 19 hours and 5 minutes; a record. But this development of a yacht designed particularly with off-shore racing in mind was at the time an isolated case. Most British yachtsmen who went off-shore to race continued to do so in the older type of cruiser.

The first sign of a change came in 1928, when the Fastnet race of that year was won by a schooner called *Nina*. Designed for Mr. Paul Hammond by Starling Burgess, *Nina* was the first of the true off-shore racers from America. She won the transatlantic race to Spain and followed this by winning the Fastnet so effectively as to cause what can only be seen in retrospect as a storm of jealous criticism. In point of fact *Nina*, although built specifically for ocean racing, had certain exaggerated features in her design which were not copied by subsequent vessels in spite of *Nina*'s outstanding success in off-shore racing. The vessel which really set the fashion was *Dorade*.

Dorade, far from being an eccentric vessel like *Nina*, looked to English eyes perfectly normal. In some ways she resembled an eight-metre. This was not entirely surprising, for her designer, young Olin Stephens, had been designing successful six- and eight-metre yachts to the International Rule for some time. Rigged as a yawl, *Dorade* won the transatlantic race and the Fastnet in 1931, and the Fastnet again in 1933. She truly marked the start of a new era in off-shore racing. 1935 produced the most successful Fastnet race to date. There were seventeen

starters, thirteen of which were British, three French and one American. The American was a new yawl designed by Olin Stephens called *Stormy Weather*. Three of the British yachts could be said to be of the new ocean racing type, one of them being the elegant blue *Foxhound* designed by C. E. Nicholson and built by Camper and Nicholsons. *Stormy Weather* was the winner.

Boats designed by Olin Stephens and skippered by his brother Rod had won three successive Fastnet races; *Dorade* in 1931 and 1933 and *Stormy Weather* in 1935. Far from demoralizing English owners and designers this acted as a spur, and enthusiasm for the Fastnet race (and for ocean racing generally) grew. For the 1937 race eighteen British yachts came to the line and in 1939 Charles Nicholson, with a new yawl *Bloodhound*, produced the winner, but it must be admitted that there was no American competition that year. It must also be recorded that the owner for whom Camper and Nicholsons had built both *Foxhound* and *Bloodhound* was an American, Ikey Bell (an expatriate spending most of his time in the British Isles). *Bloodhound* raced in the 1960s (under the ownership of Her Majesty Queen Elizabeth). *Stormy Weather* was beamier and a more powerful yacht altogether than *Dorade*, but both these boats, perhaps particularly *Stormy Weather*, representing as she did the vanguard of American thinking in off-shore racing, were to have a marked influence on the future style of the 'ocean racer'. With *Foxhound* in 1935 the powerful reputation of Charles E. Nicholson was behind the new off-shore cruiser-racer. But two new designers had come on the scene—Robert Clark and J. Laurent-Giles. From the board of Robert Clark came *Ortac* while Laurent-Giles designed the then daring *Maid of Malham* for John Illingworth, who was later to achieve a remarkable series of wins in a series of equally remarkable yachts.

These two vessels really set the trend for the new British boats. By 1938 there were no less than thirty Royal Ocean Racing Club races that summer; the longest being from Dover to Kristiansand; some 488 miles. Furthermore, it was by no means only the British who were building boats. Those countries which border the Channel, the North Sea and the Baltic, Norway, Sweden, Germany, Holland, Belgium and France, were all to be intrigued and involved in the new sport of ocean racing. The Heligoland race of 1938 serves well as an example. Thirty-eight yachts came to the line, of which eighteen were Germans, sixteen British and four Dutch. Of the German boats, five were owned by the Luftwaffe and two by the German Navy; the rest were privately owned, apart from one *Hamburg* which belonged to the Hamburgischer V.S. The race was won by the British yacht *Ortac* designed by Robert Clark and owned by C. F. King, D.S.O., M.C.

American Harry Pidgeon's Islander, *a yacht he built himself and sailed round the world.*

The French tennis player Alain Gerbault's yacht Firecrest *in which he crossed the Atlantic.*

A story related some years ago to the author by the late Cuthbert Mason tells of one of these prewar ocean races when crossing tacks with a yacht owned by the German navy. Both yachts being double reefed and oilskins very much the rig of the day, Mason was surprised to see through the windows of a deck-house, the German yacht's crew sitting down to a substantial dinner at a steeply heeled table wearing full naval mess kit.

This story of Cutty Mason's is probably out of place in a history but to borrow from Ernest Hemingway it . . . 'may be regarded as fiction . . . but there is always the chance that such . . . fiction may throw some light on what has been written as fact'. The Germans, in whatever rig, were keen and successful ocean racers and such designers as Henry Gruber of Germany were producing fine examples of the off-shore cruiser-racer before the war.

The Cruising 'Bug'

While, in the period between the wars, class racing was suffering changes and the new sport of off-shore racing was expanding, there was a rapidly increasing number of yachtsmen for whom the lure of the blue horizon was infinitely more preferable to arriving at a given place ahead of a whole lot of other yachts. More and more people were discovering the charm, the escape from the work-a-day world and the sense of adventure produced by even a short coastal cruise. But if there were many for whom coastal hops, relieved by the occasional longer sea passage during a holiday, was sufficient, there were others in whom the fatal bite of the cruising bug induced such wanderlust that we find a number of very long distance cruises being made in the between-wars period. In 1920 G. H. P. Mulhauser, an Englishman, began a voyage which took him 31,000 miles round the world in the 37-ton yawl *Amaryllis.* In 1924 the tennis-playing Frenchman, Alain Gerbault, crossed the Atlantic in the 39-foot cutter *Firecrest,* a British cutter built in 1892. In 1928 an American, William Albert Robinson, sailed round the world in the 32-foot ketch *Svaap,* some of the time with a Tahitian named Etera as crew. In 1930, Ahto Walter, an Esthonian, began a series of five crossings of the Atlantic, the last to be in 1932. All in all Ahto Walter sailed some 25,000 miles. In 1934 the Royal Cruising Club awarded the Club Challenge Cup to Commander R. Graham R.N. for his cruise in the 8-ton *Emanuel.* In 1934 A. G. H. McPherson made an Atlantic crossing in *Driac II.* And the list could continue. Perhaps one of the more remarkable things about these people is that they were not only exceptional seamen, they were authors as well, and Mulhauser, Gerbault, Robinson, Graham and McPherson all wrote excellent accounts of their voyages.

The period between the two world wars also saw changes in the world of the power yacht. It saw the end of the steam yacht and the development of two classes which replaced it: the diesel and the petrol yacht.

The first diesel yacht had been built by Camper and Nicholsons in 1913 and called appropriately, *Pioneer.* This large vessel, 163 feet in length, 24 feet 6 inches in beam, was built for Mr. Paris Singer. Two-hundred-and-fifty horse power Atlas Polar diesels built in Copenhagen provided her power. In 1917, Camper and Nicholsons also built *Ara* for the French Navy. A larger ship than *Pioneer,* some 213 feet on the waterline, *Ara* mounted two guns. Her war service over, she caught the eye of the American, William Vanderbilt. It was love at first sight and in 1922 Vanderbilt bought her from her owner, Captain Heriot.

The main advantage of the diesel yacht was that the space taken up by the engines was greatly reduced. Secondly, diesel oil was cheaper. Of the two principal British builders of luxury yachts, Camper and Nicholsons and G. L. Watson of Glasgow, the latter seem to have been slower to adapt to diesel, and continued to build huge steam yachts right up to the early Thirties. Furthermore the Camper and Nicholsons yachts became increasingly functional in appearance whereas the Watson yachts retained the features of the prewar steam yachts. However, many of the Watson yachts, which combined the elegant but now obsolescent stylistic features of the steam yacht with diesel propulsion, were extremely successful; for example Major Stephen Courtauld's *Virginia,* built in 1930. *Virginia* was a large vessel of her kind, measuring 209 feet overall. She had the long-drawn-out counter of the old steam yacht, in contrast to *Ara,* a much older boat, with her straight stem, functional stern and absence of traditional elegance. *Pioneer* combined a reasonably graceful counter stern with an uncompromising straight stem. *Sister Anne,* a Camper and Nicholsons yacht built in 1929, was another vessel completely functional in appearance. American diesel yachts followed the same pattern. In 1928 Theodore Ferris of Cox and Stevens Inc. designed *Nourmahal* for Mr. Vincent Astor. She was built by F. Krupp in Germany (along with many other American diesel yachts). It was cheaper for Americans to build in Germany.

One of the best-known and one of the most luxurious motor yachts ever built was *Philante,* the 263-foot overall, 1,628-ton gross, motor yacht which Camper and Nicholsons designed for Sir T. O. M. Sopwith. *Philante* had a cruising speed of 14 knots and a range of 7,000 miles. (She now knows service as the Royal Norwegian Yacht *Norge.*) Although the First World War had brought inflation, the 1930s were to see a large number of huge motor yachts being built. A good example is *Shemara,* built in 1938 for Sir Bernard Docker. *Shemara* is 212 feet in overall

Motor Yachts

Ara, the second diesel yacht; built originally in 1917 for the French Navy, she was bought in 1922 by Mr. William Vanderbilt.

Shemara, designed and built by J. I. Thorneycroft and Co. for Sir Bernard Docker. Shemara is now owned by Mr. Harry Hyams.

Virginia, built in 1930 for Major Stephen Courtauld. With the long overhangs, clipper bow and bowsprit of the old time steam yacht, she makes a graceful picture.

Nourmahal. Designed in America for Mr. Vincent Astor, Nourmahal was built in Germany by F. Krupp.

length and was designed and built by J. I. Thorneycroft and Company Ltd. of Southampton. With *Philante* and *Shemara* a compromise had been reached in design between the square functional appearance of a vessel like *Sister Anne* and the long elegant overhangs of *Virginia* and we find in both *Shemara* and *Philante* a pleasing sheer-line terminating in a sharp eager-looking bow, with exactly the right amount of overhang. But these huge, luxurious vessels represent only a small part of the picture. The period between the wars saw great expansion in the number of small motor cruisers the world over, many of them based on work boats, others tending to be imitations in miniature of their large sisters. Although there were pleasing exceptions, their general appearance by modern standards was ungainly. However, just as the modern cruising sailing yacht owes much of her stylish appearance to the effect of the needs of racing upon designers, so the general demands of streamlining in motor boat racing were to bring about, over the years, much improvement in the design of small motor cruisers.

Pioneer, *the first diesel yacht designed and built by Camper and Nicholsons in 1913.*

Bluebird I, *Sir Malcolm Campbell's record breaking single-step hydroplane. Designed by Fred Cooper and built by Saunders Roe Ltd., she had a twelve-cylinder Rolls-Royce engine giving 2,150 h.p. Her record speed was 130 miles per hour.*

Philante, *originally owned by Sir T. O. M. Sopwith. She is now the Norwegian Royal Yacht* Norge. *Small pictures show the saloon and owner's stateroom.*

Sir Malcolm Campbell standing behind Bluebird II.

above:
Miss America*'s* VII *and* VIII *with which Gar Wood defeated the challenge of British yachtswoman, Miss Betty Carstairs.*

Maple Leaf IV *designed and built by S. E. Saunders in 1912. This historic vessel was the first in the world to reach a speed of 50 knots.*

Gar Wood and Olin Johnson, his mechanic. Gar Wood called his boats Miss America. *He was a very successful American racing motor-yachtsman of the 1920s.*

Motor Boat Racing

This is not as modern a sport as might be imagined. As far back as 1902 a marine motoring association had been formed for the purpose of controlling British Motor Boat racing. On 8 April 1908, a patent was taken out by a certain William Henry Fuber. This was one of nine British patents between the years 1906 and 1909. The patents were British but Fuber was an American, living in France. He was one of the pioneers in the history of hydro-planes. In the early part of the twentieth century a British designer, S. E. Saunders, had also designed and built a number of single-step hydro-planes. The 1908 patent which Fuber took out had seven steps in a straight line, all of equal power. Saunders applied his own theories to this patent, reducing the steps from eight to five and, instead of the flat bow designed by Fuber, he substituted a convex 'V-section' bow. The boat to emerge was called *Maple Leaf IV*. She is historic as being the first boat in the world to reach a speed of 50 knots, defeating the Americans and other comers in the 1912-13 races for the British International Trophy or as it is also known, the 'Harmsworth Trophy'.

The firm of John I. Thorneycroft and Company (the builders of *Shemara*), were also turning out hydro-planes in the early part of the century. Before the First World War, Monaco was a great place for power-boat racing, and in 1910 Tom Thorneycroft raced his *Miranda IV* which unlike *Maple Leaf* was a single step hydro-plane. Based on this were the coastal motor boats which Thorneycrofts built for the British Navy during the First World War. The design was submitted in the early summer of 1915 and by January of the following year twelve boats had been ordered and work started. Construction was extremely light, using laminated frames with spaced members in between to give strength. All were built in wood. These fast 'coastal motor boats' with their great ability at sea (in most weathers) were to contribute markedly to the knowledge of those who were to be much occupied with the problems of building similar, if more advanced, craft in the years to come.

In the early Twenties the Americans staged two pioneering off-shore power-boat races: one a 350-miler from Boston to New York, and the other 250 miles around Long Island. Also in this period was held the first Albany to New York race: 133 miles, in memorably bad weather.

The first off-shore outboard power boat race in British waters took place in September 1928. These outboard power boats were hydro-planes, descendents of the Thorneycroft boats. The hulls were of the lightest possible construction; designed to skim over the surface of the water, propelled at the maximum speed by the minimum power; designed to plane or travel over the surface of the water rather than through it. In 1928 a determined challenge was made for the British International Trophy by a wealthy yachts-woman, Miss Betty Carstairs. This cup had been last won by the American Gar Wood in 1920. For the new race Miss Carstairs commissioned S. E. Saunders Ltd. to build two challengers; *Estelle I* and *Estelle II*. The designer was F. Hyde-Beadle and both boats were single-step hydro-planes. In this race, the overall length of boats was limited to 40 feet. The race was to be held at Detroit, in fresh water. Determined to

Niagara, an American 'speed' steamer.

Oma, British experimental hydro-plane, using air screw.

hold his trophy, Gar Wood entered not only the reconditioned *Miss America* but *Miss America VI, Miss America VII* and *Miss America VIII,* the latter with a single Packard 800 horsepower motor. A formidable riposte! *Estelle II* capsized in the first race and Gar Wood emerged the winner in *Miss America VII* at the awesome speed of just under 93 miles an hour.

Most of the high-speed boats of the Twenties and Thirties followed the principle of the hydroplane. This included the vessels built to capture the world's speed record on water. The two *Bluebirds* of Sir Malcolm Campbell were single-step hydro-planes. However, the stepped hull design began to give way in the 1930s to what are known as 'displacement hulls'. The term displacement is used here to mean a hull which, in order to float, displaces water equal to its own weight. Of course displacement hulls were the common form of the larger type of motor boat. But in high-speed racing it presented new problems. The pioneer of displacement hulls for power vessels was to be S. E. Saunders. We have already seen how in the years before the war Saunders was building high-powered displacement hulls to race in the Mediterranean waters off Monte Carlo, chiefly against the French and Italians. We have also seen how he came to design *Maple Leaf IV* in 1912, and we saw how although *Maple Leaf* was a stepped hull, Saunders had gone further and, in order to increase the lift given by the stepped hull, produced the 'chine' form. The new and pronounced 'V-section' ended in a short stem which had the effect of lifting the bow immediately the boat moved ahead, the lift increasing with the speed

of the boat. This form of design is still used today in a modified form—evidence of how far Saunders was ahead of his time.

Another British designer who contributed much to the sport of motor boat racing was Hubert Scott-Payne with his British Power Boat Company at Hythe on Southampton Water. He developed the hard-chine principle in his larger craft, improving upon Saunders' ideas. In the early Thirties he was producing a range of fast motor boats from 25 to 50 feet, powered by a variety of engines. Scott-Payne's power boats enjoyed a tremendous vogue in the Thirties. The technical expertise of Hubert Scott-Payne of the Power Boat Company and of Peter du Cane of Vospers Ltd. were of vital importance in the design and production of Motor Torpedo Boats, Motor Gun Boats and Air Sea Rescue vessels in the Second World War. All of these vessels made use of the chine principle. They were powered by petrol engines in contrast to their equivalent, the German E-Boats, which were powered by diesel engines of a precision and reliability which at the time the Allied Navies seemed unable to match. The E-Boats were slower however than the fastest of the M.T.B.s (an approximate maximum of about 35 knots to the British vessels' 40). Much research was done by the designer John Hacker in the Second World War. He experimented particularly in what is known as 'rise of floor' in such vessels. The principle of this is that the more rise there is in the floor of a vessel throughout her length the easier will she cut through the waves—a theory which formed the basis of the extremely successful postwar designs of the American, Ray Hunt.

Ankle Deep *and* Baby Reliance, *early U.S. Hydroplanes.*

Peter Pan Jnr. *An early U.S. 'gasoline-engine driven auto-boat' —possibly not sufficiently fast to ruffle the large hats of the two fair passengers!*

left:
A Royal Navy motor torpedo boat.

YACHTING SINCE 1945

Smaller Boats, New Materials and Electronic Aids

'He that contemneth small things shall fall by little and little.'
Ecclesiasticus, 19:1

The America's *Cup.*

In the yachting scene after the Second World War certain trends, discernible in the period between the wars, have become established. In the case of the racing sailing yacht the classes of large boats have declined, while the smaller keel boats like 'Dragons' and national and local One-Design classes have increased; as have the number of dinghy classes: this being the biggest increase of all. Shortly after the war, the 'Dragon' class acquired royal prestige when the Island Sailing Club of Cowes presented one (subsequently named *Bluebottle*) as a wedding present when Her Majesty the Queen (then the Princess Elizabeth) married Prince Philip. The Duke of Edinburgh has since been an active participant in yacht racing in classes like the 'Dragons' and the Uffa Fox-designed 'Flying Fifteens'; and again following royal tradition, is President of the R.Y.A. In racing in the small boats Prince Philip follows the trend of class racing today. The metre boats have become virtually obsolete, apart from the 12 metres, in which vessels the *America's* Cup is now raced.

The introduction of new materials largely brought about by the war, such as aircraft alloys, resin-bonded plywood and the subsequent enormous development of glass reinforced plastics have led to a revolution in yacht building. And today a number of yachts have been successfully built in ferro-concrete. The *America's* Cup rules have recently been modified so that the contending 12 metres may be built in aluminium, and in time other newer lightweight materials of the space age will doubtless come into general use in yachting. Man-made fibre has replaced hemp and other rope materials. It was not long in the postwar period before nylon and terylene sails had replaced canvas, and there are now a variety of species of this man-made fibre. Because of inflation, these trends have not necessarily made the sport of yachting cheaper. The enormous growing popularity of the sport in some instances tends to push up the price; for example, to accommodate the growing fleets of yachts of every kind, 'marinas' or artificial yacht harbours have been built in almost every country in the world. To remunerate those who finance these projects, the cost of moorings has risen. Boats can be built more quickly using fibre-glass strengthened plastics which are cast in moulds; like, for example, the moulds made by 'Halmatic' which are from the designs of Camper and Nicholsons and which are subsequently completed by Camper and Nicholson; and fine little vessels they make; but this is singling out one among many firms producing vessels to suit every taste and pocket and literally the world over.

In the field of aids to navigation, the electronic inventions of the Second World War (radar for example) have been improved and modified for yacht usage. Radio Beacons aid the navigator; Radio Telephone keeps the deep-sea cruiser in touch with the shore. Echo-sounding machines give him the depth of water (within soundings) in which he is sailing at the flick of a switch. The modern navigator has many devices to assist him in his art. All these electronic aids are however, only 'aids' and do not replace the time-honoured methods of navigation.

The 1958 series. The first in 12 metres. The crew of Columbia, *the successful defender, cheer* Sceptre. *She had gamely finished the course with a broken boom (temporarily repaired).*

Changes in the *America's* Cup Rules

Wars bring high taxation and inflation. One of the events which had to be amended in order to survive was the *America's* Cup. After much discussion and cogitation the New York Yacht Club obtained legal permission to alter the deed of gift of the Cup. First of all the minimum waterline length was lowered to 44 feet, thus making the cup eligible for competition in 12-metre yachts. Secondly, the challenger need no longer cross the Atlantic on her own bottom and thirdly the challenger had the right to substitute another yacht for the one named in the challenge up to one week before the first race. By the same token the defender must be named one week before the first race.

Challenges from Britain, Australia and France for the *America's* Cup

After a lull of twenty years, the *America's* Cup business came once again to life with the challenge in 1957 by the Royal Yacht Squadron on behalf of Hugh Goodson's 12-metre *Sceptre*. The challenge being willingly accepted, three new American boats were ordered: *Columbia* to the design of Olin Stephens; *Weatherly* to the design of Phillip Rhodes and Raymond Hunt's *Easterner*. In addition, Vanderbilt's old boat *Vim* was fitted out. The new boats seemed very small by comparison with the 'J' class. Indeed the latter were twice the size (135 feet overall ('Ranger') as against the 69 feet of a 'twelve'). But by modern standards the new boats were both big and expensive. The Americans chose *Columbia* to defend the cup. She had Briggs Cunningham at the helm and the formidable combination of Rod and Olin

British America's *Cup challenger* Sceptre *working up at Cowes.*

Stephens in her knowledgeable crew, also Henry Sears, who headed the syndicate that was footing the bill. The British boat, *Sceptre*, was designed by David Boyd and helmed by Lieutenant-Commander Graham Mann R.N.

It was soon clear that the Americans had the better boat. At the start of the first race, Cunningham took up a safe leeward position ahead of the challenger. As the boats worked their way up the windward leg of the course, it was seen that *Sceptre* could not match the defender which was sailing closer to the wind and footing faster than the British boat. *Columbia* won the race by 7 minutes and 44 seconds.

Whatever the weather, and it varied sufficiently to give the challenger every chance, the story was the same in essence. However, local experts considered that tactically Graham Mann made few mistakes. It was generally agreed that *Sceptre* would have been beaten by any of the 12 metres which had been competing in the pre-cup trials. Mann emerged a popular skipper. In the fourth race *Sceptre* cracked her boom in strong winds, but Mann, although trailing by eight minutes, braced the spar and gamely continued, to finish the race.

The next challenge came from Australia with *Gretel* in 1962. The Royal Sydney Yacht Club challenged on behalf of a syndicate of Australian businessmen headed by Sir Frank Packer. As a trial horse they chartered *Vim*, Vanderbilt's prewar but extremely successful 12 metre. Indeed so fast was *Vim* in trials for the defender of the cup against the British challenge in *Sceptre* in 1958 that Bus Mosbacher had come within an

Weatherly, *the successful U.S. America's Cup defender against Australia in the 1962 series, close-hauled in conditions that give us a good idea of the seas that run off Newport.*

Sail changing aboard the Australian Challenger Gretel *in the 1962 America's Cup series.*

ace of having *Vim* chosen rather than one of the new postwar yachts. *Gretel* was the first 12 metre to be built in Australia. Her designer was Alan Payne and she was built in the Lars Halvorsen and Sons yard at Ryde. The Americans this time chose *Weatherly* as their defender. Modified and improved by Bill Luders, her builder, she had established her right at the trials to defend the cup.

It looked like being a good series. The Australians had taken immense trouble with *Gretel*. On 15 September, the day of the first race of the series, *Gretel* came to the line with Jock Sturrock as helmsman while Bus Mosbacher was helming *Weatherly*. Conditions were blustery with an 18-knot wind. The Australian yacht, hampered by parted rigging, lost this race. The second race provided even heavier conditions, but the Australian boat seemed better suited to these. After rounding the last mark of the course in a straight run to the finishing line, *Gretel* was first to hoist her spinnaker. While *Weatherly* was still hoisting hers, *Gretel*, coming up on the American's weather quarter, took the latter's wind and roared by to win with a 47 second lead. This victory, the first by a challenger since *Rainbow* was beaten by *Endeavour* in 1934, produced a rapturous welcome for the crew. But the celebrating was premature. In the third race the wind was light and variable. The conditions suited *Weatherly* perfectly and she won, crossing the line 8 minutes 40 seconds ahead of the Australian. Leading now two to one, *Weatherly* again took the lead in the fourth race,

a race which provided good tacking duels. It was a close thing. At the finishing line only 26 seconds separated the first boat home from the second; but that first boat was *Weatherly*. In the fifth race and the last one in the series, Mosbacher established a lead and hung on to it and America retained the cup.

In 1964 the British challenged again with Anthony Boyden's *Sovereign*, designed by David Boyd. The American defender was *Constellation*, designed by Olin Stephens. This series was unhappy from the British point of view. In the second race *Constellation* was to cross the line 20 minutes 24 seconds ahead of the British boat, a feat which had not been equalled since 1886. There were two potential challengers to start with: Anthony Boyden's *Sovereign* and the two Australian brothers, Frank and John Livingston's *Kurrewa V* under charter to the Englishman, Owen Aisher. Both ships were Boyd-designed. After trials *Sovereign* was selected. Her helmsman was Peter Scott.

The *Constellation* syndicate, headed by Walter Gubelmann, chose for helmsman Robert Bavier Jr, Rod Stephens going along as navigator. The series showed the marked superiority of the defender which was amply demonstrated during the very first race. The British press criticized the helmsman, but the Americans criticized the designer. But it is easier to criticize than sail a 12 metre against what has been proved to be the most formidable combination of designers, sailmakers, tacticians, helmsmen and crews in the world.

Bus Mosbacher; skipper of Weatherly; *a very experienced helmsman.*

right:
Olin and Rod Stephens—two Americans who are possibly the best-known designer-sailormen in the world.

All hands flat on deck up to windward, aboard Gretel.

left:
Aerial shot of Dame Pattie *and* Intrepid.

Gretel II *and* Intrepid. *Another Australian challenge.* Intrepid *helmed by Bill Ficker defeated Australian helmsman Jim Hardy's efforts to win the cup—but only just!* Gretel II *proved a fast boat.*

Dame Pattie, Gretel *and* Vim *during pre-cup trials.*

Intrepid *tacks ahead of* Dame Pattie.

In 1967 the Australians challenged again. Sir Frank Packer, with the Royal Sydney Yacht Squadron, made a second bid with a new twelve, *Dame Pattie*; but this too proved to be abortive. However, in 1970, a twelve from the board of designer Alan Payne came nearer to winning the trophy than any yacht since *Endeavour*. The new boat *Gretel II* had first to undergo eliminating trials with *France* a French defender backed by Baron Bich. *Gretel II* won the right to challenge the Americans, but it was a close contest. The Australian boat was helmed by Jim Hardy. A Californian architect, Bill Ficker, helmed *Intrepid*, the defender. Although *Gretel II* showed that she could outsail *Intrepid*, Ficker managed to retain the cup, demonstrating great ability to fight back and turn a losing position into a winning one. The series produced a protest case, the decision of which by the New York Yacht Club was ill-received, bringing memories of Sopwith and (still earlier) of Lord Dunraven. One thing which emerged from the

performance of *Gretel II* was a (perhaps belated) appreciation of Marcel Bich's *France* which had come close to defeating the Australian.

And so that ornate Victorian trophy still rests in America. In 1973 another *America*'s Cup series begins. Challenges have been received from Sir Frank Packer and Baron Bich, represented respectively by the Royal Sydney Yacht Squadron and Cercle de la Voile de Paris. Also contemplating challenges are the French Yacht Club d'Hyeres and the Société de Nautique de Marseille, the Australian Royal Perth Yacht Club and the Royal Vancouver Yacht Club. Aluminium construction is permitted and Olin Stephens has confirmed that future American twelves will be built of aluminium. The old rule demanding that accommodation be provided below decks has gone, and future twelves will be pure day boats. The pace is hotting up and the challengers are increasing in number and range of nationality. The future of the *America*'s Cup has never looked brighter.

Bus Mosbacher sailing Intrepid.

Modern Olympic Classes

'Tempest' class. A modern fast two-man keelboat designed by Ian Procter.

The modern Olympic Games which were revived in 1896 and which are held in different countries in the World every four years, provide, in the sailing section, an opportunity to study International class racing at its very best. The first games after the Second World War were held in 1948 in Britain and the sailing was held in Tor Bay. The largest class there was the 6-metre class and four years later, in 1952 at Helsinki, the 6-metre boats were still there; but there was a new boat intended to replace the 6, the 5·5 metre. The 5·5 metre can be said to be the joint product of Major Malden Heckstall-Smith and Charles Nicholson. The actual formula was anything but new, having been used for the 1920 18-foot International class. Resuscitated and rejuvenated in 1949, it was to be adopted by the International Yacht Racing Union in the following year. Two years later the class was officially accepted for the 1952 Olympic Games. Largely due to inflation the boats are not as cheap as they might be. The 5·5 metre, designed as a replacement for the 6-metre class primarily because that class was becoming too expensive, today costs about £4,000. It has proved a popular boat within certain limitations. It is a 'development' class, which means that the general dimensions, while being defined by the formula, permit designers to have a certain freedom. The result of this is that although the place in the Olympic fleet of the 5·5 metre has now been given to the new 'Soling' class, yet the 5·5 metre is still a challenge to top International designers, probably the most experimental of whom is the American, Britton Chance.

The 'Soling' comes from the designing board of the Norwegian Jan Hernan Linge. It is relatively cheap at a little over £1,500. Its cheapness and its performance (it is a fast boat) found favour with the International Olympic Commission and it is now an Olympic class. Again because of its cheapness and its speed, the 'Soling' may prove a serious rival to the 'Dragon'.

The Johan Anker-designed 'Dragon', which first appeared in 1929, has long been a favourite and long been an Olympic class. Unlike the 6 and 5·5 metres the 'Dragon' is a one-design. So all 'Dragons' are theoretically the same; the only scope for the designer lying in small tolerances allowed to the builder but which in fact offer to the skilled and knowledgeable quite surprising opportunities for ingenuity.

The first fleet of British 'Dragons' appeared in 1935 on the Clyde. Enthusiasm for the new class spread rapidly and by 1939 there were a number of fleets round the coast. The 'Dragon' is of the class of boat which the Scandinavians call a 'Skerry' cruiser. It has a small cabin. Originally conceived by Anker as a boat in which two people could sail from regatta to regatta in the Baltic, sleeping on board where necessary, the cabin nowadays has virtually ceased to exist, although to comply with the class rules a small token coach roof still remains. Perhaps not unexpectedly the Scandinavians tended to dominate the class. In the 1952 Olympic games for example, the Gold Medal was won by Norway and the Silver by Sweden out of a fleet of seventeen entrants. The British have had their successes, collecting the European Championship in 1963 and again in 1965. The domination of the Scandinavians in the class was broken eventually by the Americans who, winning the World Championship in 1967, went on in the following year to win the Gold Medal at

Acapulco. The 'Dragon', originally submitted by Anker as a design in a competition organized by the Royal Yacht Club of Gothenburg, is still enormously popular, and there are fleets all over the world; north and south, east and west hemispheres. If as some aver, the 'Soling', though designed to replace the 5·5 metre, is going to supersede the 'Dragon', it has a very long way to go to catch up.

Perhaps the most international boat of all is the third Olympic keel-boat class, the 'Star'. The international aspect is emphasized if we look again at the 1952 Olympic Games results, when out of twenty-one entrants, the Gold Medal was won by Italy, the Silver by the United States and the Bronze by Portugal. The 'Star' is an American product. Designed way back in 1911 by Francis Sweisguth, the original 'Star' had gaff rig. Though a heavy boat, it was cheap. It was, and has continued to be, purely a racing machine. The 'Star' is 22 feet 7½ inches overall as opposed to the 'Dragon's' 29 feet.

Coming down slightly in scale, two exciting and successful relative newcomers are the 'Flying Dutchman' and the 'Tempest'. To take the 'Tempest' first (as being a 22 footer it is nearer in length to the 'Star' than the 19 foot 10 inches 'Flying Dutchman') we see a two-man keel-boat designed by Ian Proctor. The 'Tempest' has been designated eventual Olympic successor to the 'Star'. Though both boats are fast (and wet) there are distinct differences. In the 'Star',

International 'Dragons' at Copenhagen—a class designed in 1927 by Johan Anker and still enormously popular.

The Norwegian-designed 'Soling' class.

helmsman and crew lie flat on the deck with their legs hanging over the weather rail. With the 'Tempest', helmsman and crew follow more normal racing dinghy procedure, and the crew, by being slung on a trapeze wire attached to a body-belt and leading to a point up the mast, is enabled literally to stand with his feet on the weather side of the boat, leaning out horizontally. The 'Tempest' at about £950 is cheaper than a 'Star' at about £1,500. The 'Tempest' has a fin and bulb keel.

The 'Flying Dutchman' on the other hand, is a centre-boarder designed by U. Van Essen of Holland in 1957. This boat also makes use of a trapeze for the crew. It is a very fast boat indeed, demanding great physical fitness to sail it. An excellent example of fitness, team work and superb sailing techniques in this class was seen in the performance of British yachtsmen Rodney Pattisson and David Hunt, who at Acapulco won an Olympic Gold Medal. At the time of writing they are currently the Olympic Gold Medallists. This last-mentioned craft emphasizes the current trend towards smaller boats. And the keel yachts mentioned; the 5·5 metre, the 'Soling', the 'Dragon' and the 'Tempest' all again emphasize this trend.

There are today an enormous number of International and National dinghy classes. The best of them provide the finest competition in the world, both encouraging and developing new techniques in tuning boats before the race and in handling them during the race. Among the International dinghy classes are: 'Lightning', 'Snipe', 'Vaurien', 'International 14', '5·0·5', and 'Tornado'. There are in Britain alone, a large number of National and other classes. Not only are there large numbers of dinghy classes, there are in some of them very large fleets. Racing yachts may be smaller on the average but the floating tonnage in the world is undoubtedly larger.

'Flying Dutchman' class. Sail number K 163 is Superdocious, *British winner of the gold medal in the 1968 Olympics at Acapulco, helmed by Rodney Pattisson and crewed by David Hunt.*

Becalmed in the fog, a group of 470s.

left:
One of the pleasures of dinghy racing.

right:
A gaggle of 'Cadets'.

Multi-Hull Yachts

Another trend which may be discerned today is that connected with achieving speed through light displacement craft which are able to plane. This concept (which we have already discussed in connection with the early designs of Uffa Fox) has been (literally) broadened by the development of the multi-hull yacht.

In the right conditions, the multi-hull craft is able to attain very high speeds. It is by no means a new concept. Although craft with more than one hull have never found much favour until now in northern waters, yet in the Pacific and in parts of the Indian Ocean they have been in use for centuries. There are basically two forms: the 'Catamaran' which has two equal-sized hulls and the 'Tri-maran' which has a larger central hull supported by two smaller hulls on either side. In the reign of King Charles II of England, Sir William Petty built a twin-hulled vessel. The diarist Pepys mentions the launching of this ship, named by the King the *Experiment*, on 22 September 1663. Petty in fact built several 'double bottom' ships and was continually experimenting in naval architecture. But he was a lone prophet in the wilderness. No real interest appears to have been taken in multi-hull craft in the northern hemisphere until, in the late nineteenth century, the American Nat Herreshoff began experimenting with catamarans about 30 feet long. The cross-members joining the hulls had flexible joints at the ends so that the hulls could pitch independently while remaining parallel. With such a vessel Herreshoff beat all comers in a race run by the New York Yacht Club. However this 'machine' was barred from racing under the rules of the club and the development of catamarans effectively discouraged. In the late 1950s, Roland and Francis Prout, the sons of Geoffrey Prout who had developed a canoe business at Canvey Island, Essex, in England, pioneered with Ken Pearce, a small racing catamaran. In 1959 at a regatta sponsored by the American magazine *Yachting,* the Prout catamarans, although coming second to the American 'Tiger' Cat, nevertheless wiped the floor with the single-hull boats. The potentialities of the 'Cat' were at last fully recognized.

In the same year, the Chapman Sands Sailing Club of Essex issued a challenge to the Americans. This was not immediately to materialize but in 1961 a cup (the International Catamaran Challenge Trophy) was presented by the Sea Cliff Yacht Club of America. The rules of the International Catamaran class were recognized by the I.Y.R.U. laying down that C-class catamarans must be manned by two people, must not measure more than 25 feet in length, and must not have a larger extreme beam than 14 feet. The first series was won by Great Britain and the Trophy was defended successfully seven times by Britain; four times against American and three times against Australian challengers. In 1969 the Cup was lost to Denmark. In 1970 the Australian catamaran *Quest* won the cup from Denmark. This Trophy has long been called the 'Little *America's* Cup'. The boats which race for it may be small by comparison with their large sisters who race for the *America's* Cup but they are capable of speeds of more than 30 knots.

Lady Helmsman, *a 'C' class catamaran, consistent winner of the* Little America*'s Cup and reputed to be the fastest yacht in the world.*

Cruising catamaran Golden Cockerel.

Green Lady, *built at Cowes in 1970 for U.S. millionaire Gordon Vaughan.*

Off-Shore Racing

'When I have seen the
hungry ocean gain
Advantage on the
kingdom of the shore.'
William Shakespeare

Perhaps the clearest trend to be observed after the Second World War is that of Ocean or off-shore racing, a branch of racing which was just getting into its swing only to be interrupted by the outbreak of war in 1939. In this post-1945 period the early developments and experiments of designers like Olin Stephens can be seen to have had some far-reaching effects. The trend in design had already been apparent before the war. The two concepts: the racing boat, the boat in which everything was subordinated to speed, and the cruising boat, where sea-keeping qualities combined with reasonable comfort afloat were paramount, have over the years come together in a successful compromise. (Although some modern racers are uncomfortable by cruising standards.)

Some credit for this must go to the rule-makers. The effect of the R.O.R.C. rule has been to develop a type of yacht which is both fast and supremely seaworthy. Originally the Royal Ocean Racing Club time allowances were (up to 1935) based on distance derived from rating, using a yacht of 100 feet rating as scratch. In 1936 a time-on-time scale was introduced, each yacht being given a time correction factor (T.C.F.) derived from her rating by a formula. To find her corrected time, a yacht's elapsed time in a race is multiplied by this T.C.F.

Ocean racing is now spread over a broad front as regards size of boat. It is perfectly possible to go off-shore racing in quite a small yacht. On the other hand, the sport attracts a great deal of money. The major ocean races, some of which have been mentioned, have undoubtedly acquired a prestige which before the last war

belonged to the large class (even if obsolescent) and the restricted classes of the International Rule. The larger yachts which today compete in the many and varied races of the modern International Ocean Racing fleet, cost some thirty or forty thousand pounds to buy (and in some instances, much more); moreover annual maintenance costs to keep such an ocean racer in tip-top condition are by no means low.

Compared with yacht cruising and sheltered water yacht racing, off-shore racing is uncomfortable and at times extremely strenuous, mentally and physically, over a period of several days. To sail an ocean racer as hard as possible through days and nights, mostly without another competitor in sight, quite probably in heavy weather, in wet, cold and often crowded conditions, may seem to many to be a curious

'Shearwater' class catamaran.

'A' class racing catamaran, close-hauled, port tack.

Ocean racers Whisperer *and* Breeze
in close company.

American Eagle.

way in which to derive leisure enjoyment from such money as one can afford to spend on it. There is no doubt, even with rising costs, of the popularity of the sport; race entries themselves prove this. In 1960 there were 135 entries for the Bermuda race. In 1967 there were 139 entries for the Fastnet race. Such races produce much international competition; the Fastnet usually attracting yachts from Holland, France, Scandinavia, Belgium, Italy, America and Australia.

An off-shore racing 'trend-setter' of the late Thirties in which John Illingworth had achieved much success was the Laurent Giles-designed *Maid of Malham*. In 1947 Illingworth commissioned Giles to design a new cutter of 39 feet in length to be called *Myth of Malham*. Giles produced a clever and at the same time controversial design. *Myth of Malham* was of light displacement and light construction; she had very short overhangs and no sheer whatever, which had the effect of giving her a humped-back appearance. The American magazine *Yachting* described her as . . . 'a dreadful looking monstrosity'. For all this, the combination of Illingworth and the *Myth* proved invincible and they won the Fastnet races of 1947 and 1949 outright. The yacht also won her class in 1957. In the 1948 Bermuda race she finished fourth in her class, winning the Fleming Day Trophy for yachts under 40 foot. Illingworth's 'monstrosity' had proved to be the most successful British Ocean racing yacht since the Second World War.

Illingworth, while serving with the Royal Navy in Australia, was prominently involved in the first race from Sydney to Hobart in Tasmania. For this race (in 1945) there were nine starters (a race incidentally won by Illingworth). The Sydney-Hobart has become a popular and prestigious ocean race, attracting many overseas competitors. The race which starts traditionally on Boxing Day in Sydney Harbour, takes the fleet down the coasts of New South Wales and Victoria thence across Bass Strait, round Tasman Light and up to the finishing line across the Derwent River at Hobart. Although neither the Gulf Stream weather of the Bermuda race or the shifting head winds of the English Channel and the Western Approaches in the Fastnet Race provide easy conditions, the Sydney-Hobart race is perhaps unique in at times providing extraordinary conditions in the Harbour itself. This 690-mile-long race can produce weather varying from the hundred knot gusts of the 'Southerly Buster' to frustrating calm patches at the mouth of the Derwent River.

Although Australia is demonstrably increasing yearly as a yachting power, the Australians do not have it all their own way in the Sydney-Hobart race. In 1967 the Frenchman Eric Tabarly captured the Illingworth Trophy in *Pen Duick III* while the New Zealand yacht *Rainbow II* was the winner on corrected time. A more recent victory was that of British Prime Minister Edward Heath in *Morning Cloud* in

1970. Although, as with other ocean races, the eventual winner may, after the application of T.C.F., be by no means first, second or even third home, in the Sydney-Hobart race it is the yacht first home that the vast crowds on shore and afloat are waiting for. The Illingworth Trophy is for this first home yacht. Perhaps if the Fastnet Race finished off the London river; perhaps if the Bermuda race finished in Long Island Sound, the same huge crowds would be there waiting for the yacht first home. It is impossible to say, but the fact remains that the Sydney-Hobart race has managed to capture the imagination of a large sector of the Australian public. To the Britisher who hears little enough about the Fastnet apart from diminutive newspaper reports, the daily reporting of the Sydney-Hobart by television, radio and newspapers is quite astounding. The progress of the fleet on corrected time is broadcast regularly; the daily positions being worked out by a Sydney-based computer.

A very successful event from the point of view of stimulating international competition is the Admiral's Cup, first presented to the Royal Ocean Racing Club in 1957. Any country can send a team of three, four or five yachts of not less than 30 foot on the waterline. The Cup is a points cup; the winners being the team to score the highest number of points. The points are scored in two ocean races, the Channel Race and the Fastnet, and two races during Cowes Week for the Britannia Cup and the New York Yacht Club Trophy, respectively. The stipulation of not less than 30 foot waterline limits the Admiral's Cup competitors to classes I and II Ocean racers. However in February 1972 the Royal Ocean Racing Club announced a new international off-shore trophy for smaller yachts, provisionally to be called the North European Cup. Racing for the cup will take place in non-Admiral's Cup years and will be open to Class III, IV and V boats, that is to say 28·9 foot rating to 21 foot rating in the International Off-shore Rating Rule. Once again it is a points cup. The first-ever Admiral's Cup was won by Britain, and two years later in 1959 again by Britain, second place being taken by the Dutch team. The American team won the Admiral's Cup in 1961 and the British won it the next two consecutive times but in 1967 came the first Australian victory with the yachts *Caprice of Huron, Mercedes II* and *Balandra.*

As a result of the R.O.R.C. limiting (in its early stages) the size of yachts eligible to compete in its races, a number of enthusiasts formed the Junior Off-shore Group, a body which now regularly runs races throughout the season, starting in April and finishing at the end of September. The Junior Off-shore Group is but one of a number of Associations running races in British waters. There is the East Anglian Off-shore Racing Association, the Irish Sea O.R.A., the North East Cruiser-Racing Association, to name three others. And this is in British waters alone; there are hundreds of associations running off-shore races the world over.

It is the adoption of the new International Off-shore Rule that now makes it possible for yachts truly to compete internationally. Ocean Racing has come a long way from Thomas Fleming Day's first Bermuda Race in 1906 and a long way from the first Fastnet in 1925 but it can really now be said to have come of age with the adoption of this first real International Off-shore Rule. In the 1950s Ocean racing was controlled virtually by one of two rules: the rule of the Cruising Club of America or the rule of the Royal Ocean Racing Club of Britain. The formulae in these two rules were different. In 1960 a meeting occurred in Bremen in Germany. Here European yachtsmen emphasized the problems arising from these two differing rules. The result was the formation of an off-shore rules co-ordinating committee upon which were representatives from both the C.C.A. and the R.O.R.C. The committee met over a number of years but only minor changes were made and the two rules remained different. Ten years after the first meeting in Bremen the International Off-shore Rule which enabled yachts on both sides of the Atlantic to race under one International Rating Rule, came into being. This was partly the result of the increase on a world-wide scale of the use of the Ocean Racing Rules for every type of handicap and cruiser racing. Its formation and acceptance was also undoubtedly accelerated by the new type of sailing event; such as the British Admiral's Cup, the American Onion Patch Trophy, or the Australian Southern Cross, all of which involve teams of national yachts.

The modern off-shore racer inheriting from such widely differing ancestors as *Jolie Brise, Dorade* and *Myth of Malham,* is an efficient, and thoroughly seaworthy vessel with a sleek, functional beauty all her own. Although modern trends have to some extent unified design features (there are fashions in bows, in sheers, in counters, etc), closer examination of the scene reveals much individuality. The Australian Mr. Gwingate's *Caprice of Huron,* the Frenchman Eric Tabarly's *Pen Duick II,* the South African Mr. C. Bruynzeel's *Stormvogel,* the American Carelton Mitchell's *Finisterre,* and the tough British Admiral's Cup team of Mr. Arthur Slater's *Prospect of Whitby,* Mr. Bob Watson's *Cervantes IV* and Prime Minister Edward Heath's *Morning Cloud* bear witness to this.

The international flavour of modern cruiser/racing is growing yearly. In the next Admiral's Cup series some seventeen nations are involved. There is much interchange of ideas. The French are entering an American-designed boat in their team. Belgium is entering a British-designed and built vessel. Britain is entering American-designed and part Dutch-built yachts. 'Off-shore' is now indeed 'International'.

pages 114 and 115:
Morning Cloud—*(sail number 2468) the yacht of British Prime Minister, Mr. Edward Heath, who is at the helm).*

pages 116 and 117:
Prospect of Whitby.

Caprice of Huron, *one of the 1971/72 Australian Admirals' Cup team.*

left:
Mr. Bob Watson's Cervantes IV *(leading). Sparkman and Stevens (U.S.) designed—W. A. Souter (English) built. Typical International Off-shore Rule yacht for team and individual events in ocean racing.*

right
American cruiser/racer yacht Carina.

left:
French yachtsman Eric Tabarly's Pen Duick III.

right:
Kialoa II, *one of the 1971/72 American team for Australian 'Southern Cross' Cup.*

High seas abaft Gipsy Moth IV.

Gipsy Moth IV *in Sydney*.

Single-Handed World-Girdlers

'Ringed with the azure world, he stands.
The wrinkled sea beneath him crawls;'
Lord Tennyson

*L*ong and strenuous as many off-shore races are, yet for some wanderlust-infected yachtsmen they are clearly not long enough. The post-1945 era has seen a remarkable number of examples of single-handed sailing over very great distances indeed. The single-handed yachtsman is of course no novelty. Captain Joshua Slocum circumnavigated the world alone back at the end of the last century. What has made the exploits of people like Sir Francis Chichester and Robin Knox-Johnston different is that to the feat of circumnavigating the world they added the element of racing; sometimes against other single-handed yachtsmen, sometimes, as in Chichester's case, against the times made by other vessels, notably Clipper ships. It would seem that nowadays it is not sufficient to sail alone around the world, you have to do it quickly as well. This concept has also affected the type of vessel to be used. Sir Alec Rose's *Lively Lady* was by no means a fast ship but Sir Alec is the exception to the general rule.

It is the racing aspect which distinguishes this form of single-handed sailing from the extensive world cruises of which there are a large number going on every year, sometimes single-handed but often, as in the case of Mr. and Mrs. Eric Hiscock, with husband and wife. But this sort of ocean voyaging belongs in the realm of cruising. People like the Hiscocks or the American, William Albert Robinson, or the Frenchmen Alain Gerbault and Bernard Moitessier, have a very different philosophy of sailing from people like Sir Francis Chichester. Chichester added something else to world girdling. *Gipsy Moth IV* bore on her bows the insignia of the International Wool Secretariat and while on the passage Chichester quenched his thirst regularly from

Whitbread Beer casks; for a specially designed and built yacht like *Gipsy Moth IV* required a good deal of cash.

But it also required something else in considerable measure—courage. When he sailed from Plymouth in August 1966, Francis Chichester's intention was to beat the time taken by the wool clippers to complete the run to Australia. *Gipsy Moth IV,* the vessel which Primrose and Illingworth had designed for him, was a very large boat to be handled by one man; measuring 49 feet 9 inches overall with a beam of 10 feet 7 inches and with 854 square feet of sail area. Moreover this large vessel was not being handled by a young man but by a veteran of 65. But one thing Francis Chichester did have and that was experience of single-handed sailing over long distances. He was an excellent navigator,having had in his early days experience of flying and navigating various types of aircraft over considerable distances; aircraft each of which was called *Gipsy Moth*.

In 1960 five tough single-handers staged a race east-west across the North Atlantic. They were Chichester himself, David Lewis, Jean Lacombe, Val Howells and Colonel 'Blondie' Hasler. The race was originally 'Blondie' Hasler's idea. Hasler, an experienced ocean racing yachtsman who had enlivened the ocean racing scene in the immediate post war years by successfully racing off-shore in the decidedly cramped and extremely wet 30 square metre, *Tre-Sang,* was also the inventor of a type of self-steering gear. It was a self-steering device of this type which Chichester had fitted to the stern of *Gipsy Moth III* and which he nicknamed 'Miranda'. Since then many passages have been made employing types of steering gear. There are

Sir Francis Chichester bathing, gathering flying fish, and sitting in a chair mounted on gimbals with built-in eating trays.

Chay Blyth in British Steel.

Bernard Moitessier in Joshua, *the French entrant in the Round the World Race.*

now two principal types: the pendulum-servo type of vane gear and the 'trim-tab-type' in which the wind vane turns a small rudder (the trim-tab) which is itself hung on the trailing edge of the main rudder.

The 1960 single-handed race was won by Chichester. In 1962 he set off again, this time breaking the single-handed transatlantic record (again in *Gipsy Moth III*). His next, round-the-world, adventure (in 1966) was to prove a much tougher undertaking but he had acquired the experience for it. Francis Chichester did not succeed in beating the time of the wool clippers but he did succeed in sailing *Gipsy Moth IV* to Australia and from Australia back to England to a fantastic reception which was televised. Shortly afterwards he was knighted by Her Majesty Queen Elizabeth II in a moving ceremony at Greenwich.

Also to receive a knighthood for a similar venture was 59-year-old Portsmouth greengrocer Alec Rose who made the passage in a homely ketch called *Lively Lady*. In 1964 there had been another solo race across the Atlantic in which Chichester and Alec Rose took part. Rose too,

Robin Knox-Johnston in Suhaili.

therefore, had experience of long distance solo sailing. He set out in August 1967 with the intention of racing Chichester. But in the English Channel he was unfortunate enough to collide with a merchant ship. Having returned to Plymouth for repairs the yacht fell from the stocks in the dockyard, doing so much damage that it was impossible to repair her in time to race Chichester. Nevertheless repairs having been effected, Rose set out undeterred. Something about Alec Rose's likeable modesty and the fact that his attempt had no commercial backing caught the imagination of the public and he too returned to a large enthusiastic reception covered by television.

Probably the single-hander who exhibited the greatest *sang froid* was Robin Knox-Johnston, a 30-year-old merchant navy officer. The exploits of Chichester and Rose had resulted in a race round the world known as the Golden Globe Race. A prize of £5,000 was offered for the fastest solo circumnavigation non-stop. Knox-Johnston in *Suhaili* was the only man to finish the race.

Tragedy occurred when on 10 July the trimaran *Teignmouth Electron* sailed by Donald Crowhurst was found sailing off the Azores with no-one aboard. Considerable mystery was attached to this. After an examination of the log on board it appeared that for 243 days Crowhurst had never left the Atlantic, although thought to be sailing the course round the world. Some of the radio messages which he sent giving his position were found to be misleading and it was clear that as the voyage proceeded his state of mind was affected. What exactly happened no one knows; it is a tragedy of the sea. This race was unfortunate for the reputation of the multi-hull vessels. *Victress*, sailed by Nigel Tetley, foundered in a gale north of the Azores after

Robin Knox-Johnston aboard Suhaili.

left:
Dr. Lewis and his family aboard his boat at Plymouth.

Bernard Moitessier moors Joshua *in the harbour of Papeete, Tahiti.*

being at sea some nine months.

The French entrant Bernard Moitessier could have represented a very real challenge to Knox-Johnston but he decided to attempt a second world circuit and was sighted rounding the Cape of Good Hope. Moitessier, it seems, preferred to continue sailing round the world to collecting the prize money. A philosopher, in love with the sea and sailing, Moitessier relinquished what at the time was his lead to the tough and laconic Knox-Johnston. The latter's behaviour at a press conference, after having spent some ten months at sea, in which he gave the impression that world single-handed sailing was a simple business within the reach and capacity of anybody, did not obscure his remarkable achievement. Knox-Johnston is a very tough and able sailorman indeed. Bernard Moitessier, having dropped out of the race when in a commanding lead and having set off round

Donald Crowhurst astride the prow of his newly launched trimaran Teignmouth Electron.

the world for the second time, came finally to anchor off one of the Southern Pacific Islands.

Although the reputation of the multi-hull suffered somewhat in the Golden Globe Race, many long-distance cruises have been made successfully in multi-hulls, and the Frenchman Eric Tabarly has been tireless in trying out and developing such craft for long single-handed passages, his efforts being crowned with success in Colas' victory in the 1972 Transatlantic race.

Another single-handed competitor in the Golden Globe Race of 1968 was a young Scot, Chay Blyth. Blyth did not get further than South Africa, and sailed back to England accompanied by his wife. But the experience was invaluable, and two years later he was to make one of the most remarkable single-handed circumnavigations.

Born in Hawick, Blyth, who had joined the Parachute Regiment at 18 years of age, made his

right:
Teignmouth Electron being lowered into Santa Domingo harbour from the Royal Mail Ship Picardy which found it adrift in the Atlantic and abandoned.

Val Howells.

Eric and Susan Hiscock on board their 30-foot sloop Wanderer III.

Sir Alex Rose relaxes aboard Lively Lady.

British Steel, *the vessel Chay Blyth sailed around the world the 'wrong' way.*

Victress, *Nigel Tetly's catamaran which foundered in a gale north of the Azores.*

mark in 1966 when, with Captain John Ridgway, he rowed across the Atlantic Ocean in 92 days. He left the army in the following year, having been awarded the British Empire Medal, and took up sailing with little or no previous experience.

In 1970, leaving Hamble on 18 October, he sailed the yacht *British Steel* (finance had come from the British Steel Corporation) round the world, but—the 'wrong' way round, that is to say, west about round Cape Horn. This is traditionally the tough route, and Blyth had his share of foul weather.

British Steel, designed by Robert Clark, was 59 feet overall, and had a beam of 12 feet 10 inches and a draft of 8 feet. By comparison *Gipsy Moth IV* was 49 feet 9 inches, Alec Rose's *Lively Lady* was 36 feet overall and Robin Knox-Johnston's *Suhaili* was 32 feet overall. Both Blyth and Chichester's vessels were big for a single-hander, especially in Chichester's case as he was no youngster to be racing round the

world unaided.

Quite apart from the 'round-the-world' sailors, there have been a large number of long passages made in very small boats. In 1966 a passage from Florida to Ireland was made by Bill Verity in a 12-foot boat, *Nonalca.* Another very small vessel to cross the Atlantic was *Sea Egg,* only 11 foot 6 inches long, in which John Riding made the voyage in 1965. There have been a number of such crossings.

Mrs. Sharon Adams made a mark for the female sex by being the first woman to sail from Japan to San Diego, some 6,000 miles across the Pacific, alone in a 31 footer, a remarkable achievement. Another woman, Mrs. Ann Davison sailed alone from Casablanca to Dominica in 1952. One of the most unusual crossings of the Atlantic was that of F.B. and Elinor Carlin, two Australians, who in 1950 sailed from Nova Scotia to West Africa via the Azores, Madeira and the Canaries in a 15-foot-long amphibious jeep, called *Half Safe.*

Jean Yves Terlain.

Sketch of Pen Duick IV, *winner of the 1972 Observer Transatlantic Race.*

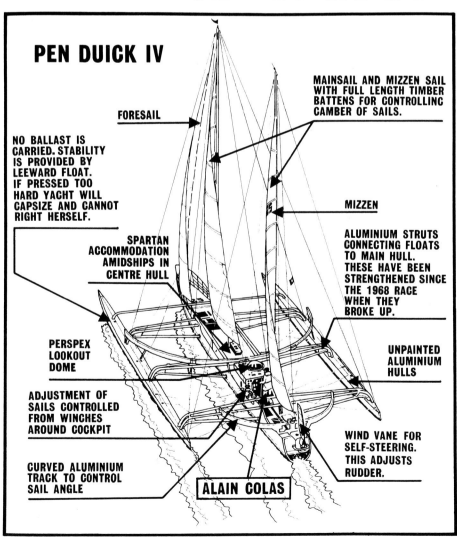

PEN DUICK IV

FORESAIL

MAINSAIL AND MIZZEN SAIL WITH FULL LENGTH TIMBER BATTENS FOR CONTROLLING CAMBER OF SAILS.

NO BALLAST IS CARRIED. STABILITY IS PROVIDED BY LEEWARD FLOAT. IF PRESSED TOO HARD YACHT WILL CAPSIZE AND CANNOT RIGHT HERSELF.

MIZZEN

ALUMINIUM STRUTS CONNECTING FLOATS TO MAIN HULL. THESE HAVE BEEN STRENGTHENED SINCE THE 1968 RACE WHEN THEY BROKE UP.

SPARTAN ACCOMMODATION AMIDSHIPS IN CENTRE HULL

PERSPEX LOOKOUT DOME

UNPAINTED ALUMINIUM HULLS

ADJUSTMENT OF SAILS CONTROLLED FROM WINCHES AROUND COCKPIT

WIND VANE FOR SELF-STEERING. THIS ADJUSTS RUDDER.

CURVED ALUMINIUM TRACK TO CONTROL SAIL ANGLE

ALAIN COLAS

*Sir Francis Chichester died on Saturday, 26 August, 1972.

left:
Victorious Alain Colas with his Tahitian fiancée at Newport after the race.

But if the reputation of the multi-hull had suffered in the 1968 Golden Globe race, the *Observer*-newspaper-sponsored Transatlantic race of 1972 was to change this. The winning yacht, *Pen Duick IV*, 70 feet long and 35 feet in beam, was a giant trimaran. The race was not without its tragedies. Veteran, one might say hero, Sir Francis Chichester, was to turn back through ill-health; a truly sad occurrence.*

The largest yacht was the schooner *Vendredi XIII* (128 feet) and the smallest was *Willing Griffin* (19 feet), a sloop entered by Englishman David Blagden. Of the entrants, 21 were British, 13 French, 5 American, 4 Italian, 3 Polish, 3 West German, 2 Australian, 1 Czech, 1 Dutch and 1 Belgian.

The winner *Pen Duick IV* averaged 5·9 knots. An all-aluminium hull, her ultra-modern looking rig had fully battened main and mizzen sails of a very high aspect ratio. Her helmsman, Alain Colas, had already had much experience of sea-going before this event. Sailed under the rules of the Royal Western Yacht Club of England, yachts of any size were eligible for the race. To qualify as a finisher, a yacht had to complete the passage, by any chosen route, from Plymouth to the finishing line at Newport, Rhode Island, by

not later than 16 August 1972. The entry of 59 closed on 17 April 1972. There were 54 starters.

The first three yachts to cross the winning line were French. Having sailed a determined and skilful race, Colas managed to beat Jean-Yves Terlain into second place. Jean-Marie Vidal in *Cap 33*, another trimaran, arrived third, while fourth home came Britisher Brian Cook in *British Steel*. When the clamour died down and the computations had been made, the following vessels and helmsmen emerged winners. Overall winner of the Observer Trophy was Colas in *Pen Duick IV* (taking 20 days, 13 hours and 15 minutes). He also collected the multi-hull handicap trophy. The winner of the monohull yachts (on corrected time) was *Blue Smoke*, sailed by Guy Hornett (taking 36 days 21 hours 16 minutes). In the under-35-foot class (on corrected time), Alain Gliksman and *Toucan* emerged victors (taking 28 days 12 hours 54 minutes). The Ida Lewis Trophy went to the First American to finish, Tom Follett, in *Three Cheers*; another multi-hull, and the Royal Western Yacht Club's Trophy for the first woman home was won by gallant Marie-Claude Fauroux, sailing *Aloa VII*. A great race. The catamarans, and the French, had reason to be pleased.

below:
Vendredi 13, *sailed by Terlain and sponsored by film producer Claude Lelouch, leaves Plymouth, the start of the race.*

Modern Cruising Under Sail

𝓕or every man or woman who sets out on a long-distance race, whether alone or with crew, there are hundreds of cruising yachtsmen who sail often remarkable distances for the sheer pleasure of doing so, without wishing to establish precedents or break records. Such cruises do not catch the public eye; they are not news. When Eric and Susan Hiscock, who twice circumnavigated the globe in their yacht *Wanderer,* arrived one time in Sydney, reporters who had come aboard were so disappointed at the lack of evidence of gales at sea and the calm and relaxed way in which the Hiscocks described their voyage that their arrival had virtually no coverage in the Sydney papers. There are many experienced ocean voyagers like the Hiscocks, and in places like Bermuda, the Azores, the Galápagos, the Marquesas Islands, Tahiti, the Fiji Islands, etc. may be found salt-stained boats whose tanned occupants have known the weather in all its moods as their small homes slice their way across the world's oceans.

Of course, cruising is not all long-distance. The successors of John North, of McMullen and of Knight abound in their thousands in the world today. Fibreglass reinforced plastic construction, production-line methods, the use of man-made fibres in sails and rope, have helped to keep inflation within reasonable bounds where small cruising boats are concerned. There is also a huge second-hand market—as a glance at any of the yachting periodicals will show. And that love of the diehard cruising man, the converted work-boat, is by no means extinct around the coastlines of the world. There is a vast fleet of converted craft of all kinds, and a whole new industry has grown up around the concept of 'do-it-yourself'. Boats may be bought in kits of parts or partially built and only wanting completion. Books on building and maintenance and courses in navigation and pilotage, all help to cater for this ever-growing world-wide navy of cruising yachtsmen. Cruising has become for many a way of life, and for thousands more it represents the ideal weekend and holiday escape.

In the anchorages of the world may be seen large enviable auxiliary sailing yachts which, being not ocean racers, must be termed 'cruisers'. Some of these are no doubt engaged in world cruises, like the American Irving Johnson's famous *Yankee,* others are just pottering about, usually anchored off a luxury resort or the kind of island whose solitude is as attractive (and as costly) as the resort. These beautiful examples of the shipwrights' art, often Italian, Greek or American, with cosmopolitan crews, constantly varnishing and washing down, are the floating holiday homes of the wealthy. They are frequently sailing under charter. Like the big diesel yachts they are expensive to run. Such a vessel is *Creole,* the elegant three-masted schooner belonging to Greek millionaire Stavros Niarchos; originally British-owned, *Creole* was designed by C. E. Nicholson and built by Camper and Nicholsons in 1927. Her registered tonnage is 257 and her Thames tonnage is 699. Her overall length is 190·33 feet. Her beam is 31 feet. Her

Mr. Stavros Niarchos's 600-ton schooner Creole.

two powerful engines give her almost as good a speed under power as her working sails. She is both an impressive and beautiful vessel.

Yet another form of cruising is that which makes use either wholly or in part of inland waterways. The writings of John Marriner who has cruised the inland waterways of Europe extensively in his 54-foot motor yacht *September Tide,* have done much to show what scope there is in this form of cruising.

The chartering to holiday-makers of yachts, frequently with the owner acting as skipper, has become world-wide big business. Large charter fleets are found in such areas as the Caribbean and the Mediterranean. The yachts are both sail and power and cater for a wide taste.

A Nicholson 38.

Motor-Sailers

*I*n connection with cruising, a postwar trend has been the development of the motor-sailer or what is sometimes called the '50/50'. This is a simple enough concept to understand. Tides being tides and the weather being delightfully unreliable (I say 'delightfully' advisedly, for who does not get bored with day after day of the same thing?) the need for some form of mechanical power in sailing vessels has long been realized. The steam yacht disguised as a full-rigged ship was a lordly example. As engines became smaller and more reliable and lighter they could be tucked away more easily in sailing hulls. An auxiliary engine has many uses. It can help out when the wind fails in a crowded harbour or anchorage; it can hold the ship's head to wind when reefing in rising winds with a shortage of crew; it enables one to keep going in a flat calm (and the flatter the calm the faster the speed under power); and when making harbour in the evening with a falling, dying breeze and an increasing foul tide, it can get you in and ashore in time for dinner and even in time for a drink beforehand.

The motor-sailer is a development of the auxiliary yacht. The purpose of the auxiliary engine is basically for the uses just listed. The normal cruiser-racer type yacht with an auxiliary engine will sail faster under sail than under power. The idea behind the 50/50 is to produce a vessel that will sail just as fast whether using the sails or the engine. This ideal is by no means always realized but in some instances it works and can be seen to work very well indeed. A large example of this is *Blue Leopard* designed by Laurent Giles and Partners; a small example is the Nicholson '38' class; a 38-foot-long motor-sailer whose 40-horse-power diesel can punch her along at 8 knots but which can acquit herself really well under sail. Motor-sailers are generally rigged as ketches. They represent for many, the perfect compromise cruising boat and today they can be seen in hundreds in the yacht harbours of the world.

A Sea Dog, a typical motor-sailer of the smaller kind.

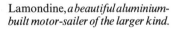

Lamondine, *a beautiful aluminium-built motor-sailer of the larger kind.*

$\mathcal{I}$n power boat racing, the postwar period has brought great expansion of the sport, both in the numbers who practise it and in the scope of their activities. There have been significant developments in engine design and manufacture, both with petrol and diesel engines. Reliability has greatly improved. In the area of hull design too, great advances have steadily been made. A typical development has been the introduction of a concave instead of convex form in the chine at the bows, eliminating the hard-hammering of the chine in rough weather. Another trend is that the after-sections, instead of being relatively flat, as they had been ever since the early days of power boat design, are deep 'V'd' like the bows, to give grip at high speed. The American designer Raymond Hunt and the builder Dick Bertram have been in the forefront of the development of this deep 'V' of an almost constant twenty-five per cent rise of floor. This form is particularly suited to a boat designed to be driven so hard that she will jump out of the water. This shape not only eases the shock of plunging back into the water but also the shock of the waves striking the ship's bottom at high speeds. Because there is some loss of both stability and lifting power such vessels are given more beam.

The Second World War effectively stopped all British power-boat racing, but it did more than that. Fuel rationing lingered on into the early 1950s. There was no proper control and organization of power-boat racing in Britain in this period, a period in which power-boating enthusiasts in Europe, and particularly America, were to acquire a significant lead. European power-boat racing was controlled by the Union Internationale Motonautique, whose headquarters were in Belgium. Britain had been represented at the U.I.M. by the old Marine Motoring Association which dated from 1902. This association had unfortunately disappeared along with the war and in the early postwar years Britain had no say in the affairs of international power-boat racing. Credit for attempting to right this situation goes to Cyril Benstead, who in 1956 founded the London Motor Boat Racing Club. This club was to become the centre of the sport in Britain. From then on other clubs sprang up wherever a suitable stretch of water could be found. Then, food and consumer goods were freed from rationing and, along with them, petrol. So began the postwar motor car boom and with it the boating boom in power-boats. This was given great additional impetus by the development of marine plywoods and glass-fibre reinforced plastics for boat building coupled with production-line techniques. In 1961 the British Power-Boat Union was formed—again on the initiative of Benstead. As the number of boats grew, there were many who considered that the proper national authority for the sport should be the Royal Yachting Association. A power-boat divisional committee of the R.Y.A.

Modern Power-Boat Racing

'The young light-hearted masters of the waves.'
Matthew Arnold

Miss Enfield, *Torquay-bound in the 1969 International Offshore Power-boat Race.*

was formed, with subcommittees for run-about racing, hydro-plane racing, off-shore racing and technical matters, thus creating a single national authority controlling the sport in Britain and with a voice in international competitions.

In 1954 Sir Max Aitken, chairman of the *Daily Express* newspaper group, joined with the Ship and Boatbuilders' Federation to hold the first International Boat Show in London. This great show, with an ever-increasing display of craft of all sizes, power and sail, is by no means the only one of its kind in the world. There are a number of similar shows, some larger than others; and just as some shows are better than other ones, so in the early boat shows. Sir Max Aitken, noticing that some of the power vessels appeared very much more seaworthy than others, decided to initiate a 200-mile race for power-boats over the open sea. This race, the forerunner of many other similar races, has undoubtedly improved the strength and sea-going ability of power-craft. In the Needles Channel the ebb-tide running against the south-west wind produces steep seas; the fleet finds races off St. Alban's Head and Portland Bill. Then there is the 50 miles of exposed sea across Lyme Bay. This race from Cowes to Torquay is a testing race and it attracts an international entry.

The winner of the 1965 race was a boat called *Brave Moppie*, designed by Raymond Hunt, built by Richard Bertram and Co. and owned and raced by Richard Bertram himself. Before Bertram took up power-boat racing he was a sailing enthusiast. When the 12-metre 'Vim' was fighting with the newly built *Columbia* for the role of defender of the *America's* Cup, Bertram was in charge of sail-handling. It was at this time that Bertram met Ray Hunt the designer, living in Miami and specializing in fast power craft capable of 30 knots in open and rough water.

After being given an opportunity to take the helm of one of these craft, Bertram now greatly enthusiastic, placed an order with Hunt for a similar boat. This, the first 31-foot vessel of single plank batten seam construction, was named *Moppie* after Bertram's wife's nickname. With a pair of 275-horse-power engines the new vessel did the measured mile at 53 miles an hour. *Moppie* went on to win the 1960 race from Miami to Nassau. Bertram stripped the engines and used the hull as a pattern for a mould from which a succession of 31-footers have been built, all of them in fibre-glass and named respectively *Glass Moppie, Lucky Moppie* and *Surf Rider*. So far the engines had been petrol driven but in 1965 Hunt and Bertram made history with *Brave Moppie*, the first diesel-engined boat to come first in a race. *Brave Moppie* was the winner of the 1965 Cowes–Torquay race. She has typical Ray Hunt lines. From her sharp bow the sections sweep outwards and downwards; the rise of floor at the midship section being about 27° and so continued to the transom aft, rise of floor at the transom being about 25°. She has a great flat deck space and her sides rise vertically from the chines, having no tumble-home at all. Before Bertram brought *Brave Moppie* to England she had done 50·1 knots (57·7 miles an hour or

above:
H.M.S. Scimitar *starts the 1971 Daily Telegraph B.P. Offshore Powerboat Race at Cowes.*

left:
Surfury *designed by Renato Levi, and owned by C. E. and R. Gardner bouncing towards victory in the 1967 International Offshore Powerboat Race.*

right:
£25,000 of Thunderfish III *goes up in smoke off Shanklin, Isle of Wight, during the 1967 Daily Express International Powerboat Race.*

92·9 kilometres). This represented the world's diesel record. She won the 1965 Miami–Nassau race as well as the Cowes–Torquay.

But if the classic off-shore races are well attended by the public, apart from the start and the finish they have small spectator value. Over a long course the boats are out of sight of one another for long distances. The small-boat men hold that the sense of strenuous competition when racing against a dozen other boats together, which comes with small outboard racing, is missing. Nevertheless, the off-shore classics attract big international entries and have their fervid supporters. In Britain off-shore power-boat racing is run in three classes: Class I, 28 to 45 feet in length; Class II, 20 to 28 feet; and Class III, to a minimum length of 14 feet. The largest class is Class III, mainly because the cost of maintenance is lower. With Classes I and II, power is limited to a maximum of 1,000 cubic inches petrol and 2,000 cubic inches diesel capacity, and there is a maximum 3,000 cubic centimetres capacity for Class III. For the big classes there are three real international events. The Cowes–Torquay for the Beaverbrook Challenge Trophy and £1,000; the Miami–Nassau in the early part of the year and the Italian Viareggio Race in the summer. These are by no means the only big races, but they have established themselves as three classics rather like the Fastnet, the Bermuda and the Sydney–Hobart in ocean racing.

The small outboard-powered craft with their 1,000 or 1,500 c/c engines towering behind them race wherever there is water—lakes, reservoirs, rivers, estuaries. These boats, capable of 70 miles per hour and more, provide some of the most exciting racing of any form in the world. Like dinghy racing it is a fast-growing sport. Whether at the London Motor Boat Club's water at Iver, Buckinghamshire or on Lake Tahoe on the California-Nevada border; whether shooting beneath the famous bridges of the Seine in the Paris 6 Heures Race or riding the open sea in the Putney (London) to Calais race, or churning up the man-made waters of the Miami Orange Bowl in Florida, the boats and the enthusiasts who practise this bucking, spray-churning method of racing over water increase in number yearly.

As might be expected, power-boat racing has an enthusiastic following in Australia; the Australian Power Boat Association is the administrative and controlling body for the sport as is the New Zealand Speed Boat Association for that country. This form of racing is also very popular in South Africa and the National Authority is the South African Power Boat Association. Most South African racing is outboard engine. Though there are many lakes and dams they are mostly small in size. This does not imply that off-shore racing does not thrive as well. There is, for example, the Cape off-shore race, 100 miles of rough Cape water, in April and another 100-mile race at Lourenço Marques.

left:
Brave Moppie, *the American winner of the 1965 Cowes Torquay Race, the first diesel-powered boat to come in first.*

right:
Lift off by Boss O'Nova II *in the 1971 race.*

pages 139-142: *start of the 1971 International Offshore Powerboat Race at Cowes.*

below:
Heavy-going in the 1971 race eliminated 25 of the 35 who started.

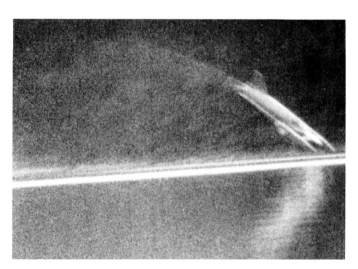

A sequence of still prints taken from a television news film showing Donald Campbell's fatal crash on Lake Coniston, 4 January 1967. The sequence shows Bluebird somersaulting at 300 m.p.h. during the attempt to beat Campbell's own record of 276 m.p.h.

Competitors in the Paris 6 hours race on the River Seine.

A Fairey 'Swordsman' fast cruising/racing offshore power-boat from Fairey Marine, a fine all-purpose vessel which can have either petrol or diesel engines.

Coronet 24 Family cruiser.

Typical sports fisherman from the well-known Bertram range of fast Ray-Hunt designed deep-V power-boat.

Two relatively recent mechanical trends have been the development of the inboard-outboard engine and of the gas turbine. There has also been much development in ignition systems. The inboard-outboard unit combines most of the advantages of both inboard and outboard units while having (allegedly) none of their vices. The inboard-outboard unit is installed through the transom and consists of an inboard engine driving through a flexible coupling to an outboard drive unit. This unit contains a reverse-reduction gearbox, steering swivel, bevel drives and propeller shaft, all of which are lubricated by an internal system under pressure. With some units, the engine cooling water is drawn in through the outdrive unit and discharged through it again with the exhaust.

It was in the Paris Six Heures race of 1966 that the first British Rover gas turbine engine appeared, driving through a Mercruiser outdrive. The boat was an American entry and lasted only a few laps before sinking; nevertheless the gas turbine development (a British enterprise) is one to watch.

Motor Cruising

Just as with sailing vessels the huge cruising fleets tend to outnumber the racing, so in the world of power-boating the same applies. The small motor cruiser, whether driven by inboard engine, by one or more outboard engines or by the relative (but highly popular) newcomer the inboard-outboard (or outdrive), is another branch of the boating industry which has expanded greatly since 1945.

There are today many associations in the world whose business it is to further the interests of yachtsmen whatever be their inclination and speciality. Looking at a list of such associations in Britain alone gives one a good idea of the scope and popularity and many-sidedness of the sport. Ranging from the Ocean Cruising Club, the Royal Ocean Racing Club, the Royal Cruising Club, the Off-shore Power Boat Club of Great Britain, with their associations of relatively deep water, to the Dinghy Cruising Association, the Inland Waterways Association, the British Canoe Union, the Association of Pleasure Craft Operators, the Hydrofoil and Multi-hull Society, the range and scope today is very wide. In order to cater for this, many firms, instead of specializing in one or two boats designed to appeal to as many tastes as possible now build a whole range of craft, each type designed to appeal to a specific section of the yachting public. There is today a vast choice which includes the type of fast off-shore power-craft known as a sports fisherman with special platforms and high steering position for deep-water fishing. At the other end of the scale, one finds plenty of little vessels carrying a small steadying sail and usually driven by diesel; general purpose and fishing cruisers for all weathers. Power-boat hulls also come in multi-hull form both for racing and general purpose.

Her Majesty's yacht Britannia.

above:
Mercury *the first gas-turbine yacht in the world, capable of over 50 knots. The property of Mr. Stavros Niarchos.*

left:
Radiant II—*built at his own yard for Mr. Basil Mavroleon. This fine ship, reputed to have cost over £400,000, is a good example of a large modern motor yacht.*

right:
Philante V, *designed by Ray Hunt of* Yachting Monthly *for Mr. Tommy Sopwith.*

Big Yachts of Today

The diesel engine, apart from driving fast racing power craft and rugged fishermen, has come into its own as the power unit of the modern descendants of the great steam yachts of the past. But not all of the postwar large yachts are diesel. Many people who know the Mediterranean have heard of (or seen) Mr. Onassis's *Christina*. *Christina* was built in 1943 by Canadian Vickers of Montreal originally as a freighter and christened *Stormont*. In 1954 Mr. Onassis had her converted and registered at the port of Monrovia. *Christina* is powered by two triple-expansion steam engines. She is shortly to be superseded by a new and completely up-to-date vessel, at present being built. Still in use after the Second World War although built in 1930 was *Nahlin*; built by John Brown and Company for the jute millionairess Lady Yule. *Nahlin* made history when the Duke of Windsor (then Prince of Wales) chartered her for an Adriatic cruise with a party of friends which included the future Duchess. *Nahlin* was probably the last yacht cast in the mould of the traditional steam yacht with long counter stern, raking masts, clipper bow and bowsprit.

In a class by herself is *Britannia*, the British royal yacht and the only royal yacht to be built since the Second World War. *Britannia* was built by John Brown and Company in 1953. Her power comes from four oil-fuelled steam turbines. Apart from her other attributes, her designers are to be congratulated on *Britannia* from a purely aesthetic point of view. Designed for conversion into a hospital ship in time of war, she combines a functional appearance with an elegance which is very pleasing.

Although the tendency in motor yacht design has certainly been towards smaller, faster boats, there are still a number of motor yachts of considerable size coming off the stocks. *Radiant II* is an example. This fine vessel (680 tons gross), is large enough to require a crew of 24. She was built in 1961 by Austin and Pickersgill in Sunderland, the yard of Mr. Basil Mavroleon, her owner. She is modern in every sense of the word; containing stabilizers and air conditioning for the comfort of crew and passengers, full radar and automatic pilot equipment and all the latest electronic devices. *Santa Maria* built in Holland in 1963 for Mr. Henry Ford by C. Van Lent is another example. *Santa Maria* is typical of the best type of modern large Dutch diesel yacht: functional, beautiful and sea-kindly. *Santa Maria* by comparison with *Norge* or *Shemara* or *Radiant* is a relatively small yacht. But for a yacht of her size even to be run and serviced properly, a wealthy owner or syndicate of owners is essential. In these days crew's wages are high and so are fuel bills. So are fitting-out and maintenance costs. Even though some economy can be effected by the ship's crew doing the painting and varnishing, nevertheless there are heavy

Philante VI, *Mr. Tommy Sopwith's recently-built motor yacht.*

costs to be borne in respect of mooring dues and charges for occupying a dry dock. And so just as with cruising sailing yachts, one of the reasons for the general reduction in size is that the smaller vessel needs fewer crew to handle her. Today in many instances that crew is comprised of the owner's friends. But there will always be some large yachts and it is well that this should be so for they are generally things of great beauty.

The Future

But what of the future? We have seen how off-shore power-boat racing has had an influence on motor yachts outside the racing scene, particularly in the question of safety equipment and engine installation. We have also seen how the American designer Ray Hunt developed the deep 'V' hull with its almost constant rise of floor. An example of how cruising yachts are influenced by racing experiments is *Philante V*, the 117-tonner built by Camper and Nicholson in 1961 for Mr. 'Tommy' Sopwith. *Philante V* is a high-speed yacht and has the deep 'V' hull form. The Italian designer Renato Levi is another who has developed the deep 'V' design. *Surfury*, owned by Charles and Richard Gardner, which came third in the 1956 Torquay race and won the 1967 Cowes–Torquay at an average speed of 53 miles per hour, makes use of Renato Levi's Delta Configuration on the deep 'V' form. With such a form, the hull, when seen in either plan from above or in profile from the side, appears wedge-shaped. In 1960 Vospers built the world's first power-yacht to make use of the gas turbine. This was *Mercury* designed by Vosper's Peter Du Cane, for Mr. Stavros Niarchos. In her trials in 1961 *Mercury* logged 54 knots. She is based on the 'Brave' class patrol boats of the British Royal Navy. By no means huge yet large enough to be extremely comfortable below, extremely fast (capable of over 50 knots), seaworthy, very streamlined in appearance, powered by gas turbine, *Mercury* is as near as we can come to visualizing the 'large' motor yacht of the future; except that the power unit may well be nuclear.

And what of the future of yachting generally? More boats everywhere, and more artificial harbours to house them seems a certain development. Racing Rules and Measurement Formulae are never perfect and will continue to be discussed and modified from time to time. New materials and methods in building hulls and making sails and all gear will appear at consecutive boat shows; and doubtless, there will be more boat shows. In all forms of yachting, the designer and the builder will be striving constantly for superior performance, and the happily sea-feverish owner will be pleased to pay for the results.

Which, apart from today's widespread availability, is how matters were with Charles II.

INDEX

Figures in *italic* refer to illustrations